Footprints of a Dream

Footprints of a Dream

The Story of
The Church for the
Fellowship of All Peoples

by Howard Thurman

WIPF & STOCK · Eugene, Oregon

Wipf and Stock Publishers
199 W 8th Ave, Suite 3
Eugene, OR 97401

Footprints of a Dream
The Story of the Church for the Fellowship of All Peoples
By Thurman, Howard
ISBN 13: 978-1-60608-451-9
Publication date 4/6/2009
Previously published by Harper, 1959

To Johanna Volkmann
  good and generous friend
  in whose life
  faith and practice
  are of
    one voice

AND

To Alfred G. Fisk
  In Memoriam

Contents

INTRODUCTION	7
PROLOGUE	11
The Social Climate in 1944—The War—The Protestant Church—The West Coast	
1. KHYBER PASS	15
My Early Years—Entering the Ministry—Experimenting at Howard University	
2. IN THIS COMMITMENT	29
Dr. Alfred G. Fisk—The Sakai Group—The Neighborhood Church—The Children's Intercultural Workshop—The Commitment—The Public Inaugural—The Move to Independence—The Types of Membership	
3. THE LETTER AND THE SPIRIT	63
The Intercultural Committee—The Pilgrimage to UNESCO—The Ministry of Music—Sunday Morning Meditation Period—The Preaching Ministry—Experiments in Adult Religious Education—The Meditation Room—Religious Education of Children—Worship through the Fine Arts—The Growing Edge Magazine—The Organizational Structure—The Use of Interns—Finances—A Church Home Is Purchased	
4. THE IMAGE OF THE CHURCH	109
The Racial Breakdown—The Membership Speaks for Itself about Itself—The Education of the Community—Funerals—Weddings—Interracial Marriages—Community Outreach—Tenth Anniversary	

5. A RADICAL TEST   131
     The Journey to Boston University—The Church Stands on Its Own Feet—Rev. Francis Geddes, the New Minister—The Program for Interns Becomes Stabilized—Stonetree Ranch Provides New Dimension of Fellowship—Conclusion

CONCLUSION   137

EPILOGUE   138
     The Social Climate in 1959—The Church Speaks Formally about Integration—Suggestions for the Local Church—South—An Illustration—North—The Negro Church

A section of photographs follows page 62

Introduction

IN THE FATEFUL DECISION of the United States Supreme Court in May, 1954, the moral initiative in the matter of democratic race relations was captured by the state. Here for the first time the highest court of the land declared that segregation was in violation of the letter and the spirit of the Constitution of the United States. This decision, as a decision, took the same position with reference to human dignity that is both implicit and explicit in the Judeo-Christian ethic, which is the theoretical cornerstone of the church as an institution in society.

It is reasonable to assume that such an institution would have through the years accumulated a body of experimental data concerning the implications of such an ethic in society. Had this been the case, the church would have been in a position to offer its cumulative wisdom to the several states in implementing the decision of the Court. The irony is that there is no such body of data available to the state. However the church is, fortunately, still in a position to offer the state specifically its all-too-recent record of successful ventures in creating Christian communities.

The story here tells of one such venture under the inspiration of the gospel of God as expressed in the teaching of the Master concerning the Kingdom of God. The story tells how a group of people in the Protestant tradition but of various backgrounds and cultures learned the meaning and the strength of an authentic religious fellowship by creating it and living within it.

The movement of the Spirit of God in the hearts of men often calls them to act against the spirit of their times or causes them to anticipate a spirit which is yet in the making. In a moment of dedication, they are given wisdom and courage to dare a deed that challenges and to kindle a hope that inspires. This was the spirit at work in Alfred Fisk and the first small band of devoted dreamers who with him formed the nucleus out of which developed The Church for the Fellowship of All Peoples. It is to his early work that I wish to pay this deep tribute.

For obvious reasons, the full story of The Church for the Fellowship of All Peoples cannot be told. What I have done is to record those events which will convey to the public mind the way in which an experiment in religious fellowship came to fulfillment. So many individuals and groups lived this story that to name them all is impossible. Even to identify certain key persons seems for the most part unwise. The conspicuous exception to this is the report of the New York Dinner held at Riverside Church in anticipation of the Tenth Anniversary Celebration.

I salute with gratitude the host of individuals whose words, labors, gifts, and prayers have sustained my own spirit through the years of this adventure and without whom the steady development of the church could not have been realized. It was my privilege to count as co-workers in the enterprise people committed to the venture as an experience in fellowship and community, the meaning of which will continue to bear fruit in the life of our times.

The persons who made outstanding contributions all along the way are numerous. Among them I list those who served as chairmen of the board of the church from 1944 to the present:

>Hugh MacMillan
>Hansel Harter
>Gene K. Walker
>Frederick Cromwell
>Donald Glover
>George Britton
>Wayne Amerson
>Clarence Johnson

All of us at Fellowship Church do express deep appreciation to Arthur U. Crosby of Philadelphia, chairman of the National Committee of Friends and Members-at-large of Fellowship Church during the crucial three-year period in which this group of individuals from far and near purchased the edifice on Larkin Street in which we now worship.

In organizing and preparing the material for this book it has been necessary to secure the help of many people—Miss Sydna

Altschuler who typed the first complete draft of the manuscript and the final draft; Mrs. Beth Ballard, my secretary at Marsh Chapel, who did much of the work in connection with the second draft of the material; Miss Ruth Coffin who provided from her own files helpful data covering certain parts of the story and who read the entire manuscript, offering many helpful suggestions; Mrs. Alice Rattner and Mrs. Jean Howard who copied single drafts; and Prof. Donald Born who gave the full scope of his technical skill in the final stages of the preparation of the manuscript for publication—to all of these I give my thanks.

The way of the pioneer is a lonely journey. For the paths on which my feet have been set, I have been blessed by the rare good fortune to have the objective thinking, counsel, and companionship of my wife, Sue, whose faith has never wavered and whose dedication to the dream is as my own.

The story has been told largely in the first person because it points out some of the landmarks on a pilgrimage which Mrs. Thurman and I began with our small daughters, Olive and Anne, many years ago when each incident along the way prepared us for the great San Francisco adventure, and for the present assignment to which we give our hearts and hands, in service to our time.

Boston
March, 1959

HOWARD THURMAN

Prologue

WHAT WAS THE CLIMATE like in America in 1944 when Fellowship Church was launched?

Our country was involved in total war. Its war aims were more negative than positive; as a nation, we knew we must destroy fascism in Europe and the Far East. The European enemy was personified in *Der Führer* of the German people. Fascism was inspired by a hard core of purpose, metaphysical in its depth and revolutionary in its dynamics. Remember how clear cut were its definitions of man, of the nature of the economic and social order which it sought to establish, and of the ultimate meaning of the good life for those who were found worthy. Pitted against fascism in this life-and-death struggle were those nations committed to various kinds and degrees of democracy. In America the commitment became increasingly definitive as it sought to oppose that clear-cut ideology of German fascism. Instead of a slogan such as "to make the world safe for democracy," which had been the rallying point for World War I, there was President Roosevelt's speech in 1941, calling for support of the Lend-Lease Bill, and for recognition of the Four Freedoms: freedom of speech and expression, freedom of every person to worship God in his own way, freedom from want, and freedom from fear. Here at last were examples which explained the precepts, the meaning of American democracy, examples the average man in America could use to evaluate his own life in this kind of country.

Even a cursory look at the contemporary scene of the period is most instructive. Segregation of the races was a part of the mores, and of the social behavior of the country. The Federal government's attitude is apparent if we state two facts:

First, all of the armed services were segregated. This segregation was given, therefore, the official sanction of the Federal government.

Second, the District of Columbia, which is in a sense a Federal reservation, the direction of which is the immediate responsibility of the Federal government, was an effectively segregated community. The schools for Negroes and whites were separate. In almost every instance the public worship of God was separate. With the possible exception of the railroad terminal and one or two other places covered by special arrangement, all public restaurants and eating places were closed to Negroes. All hotels were closed to Negroes except under rare and highly specialized circumstances. Regarding segregation there was no difference between Washington, D.C., and Atlanta, Georgia, except in public transportation. (The Supreme Court of the land had not yet seen fit to take a stand against segregation as a practice at variance with the spirit and the letter of the Constitution of the United States. In other words, not only through the South was there segregation by law, but in the other parts of the country the public temper was in favor of segregation by practice and by informal agreement.)

What was the picture in the Protestant Christian church during this period? I cannot do better than to quote three paragraphs from Loescher's *The Protestant Church and the Negro:* [1]

This is the picture which emerges: There are approximately 8,000,000 Protestant Negroes. About 7,500,000 are in separate Negro denominations. Therefore, from the local church through the regional organizations to the national assemblies over 93 per cent of the Negroes are without association in work and worship with Christians of other races except in interdenominational organizations which involve a few of their leaders. The remaining 500,000 Negro Protestants —about 6 per cent—are in predominantly white denominations, and of these 500,000 Negroes in "white" churches, at least 99 per cent, judging by the surveys of six denominations, are in segregated congregations. They are in association with their white denominational brothers only in national assemblies, and, in some denominations, in regional, state, or more local jurisdictional meetings. There remains a handful of Negro members in local "white" churches. How many? Call it one-tenth of one per cent of all the Negro Protestant Christians in the United States—8,000 souls—the figure is probably much too large. Whatever the figure actually is, the number of white and Negro persons who ever gather together for worship under the auspices of Protestant Christianity is almost microscopic. And where interracial

[1] The Association Press, New York, 1948, pp. 76–78.

worship does occur, it is, for the most part, in communities where there are only a few Negro families and where, therefore, only a few Negro individuals are available to "white" churches.

The same pattern appears to be true for other colored minorities, that is, Japanese, Chinese, Indians, Mexicans, Puerto Ricans. Regarding the Mexicans and Puerto Ricans, for example, a director of home missions work in a great denomination says his experience leads him to believe that "generally there is little, if any discrimination here though in a community which has a large Mexican population it is quite true that they have their own churches."

What was the picture on the West Coast and particularly in San Francisco during this same period? The percentage of foreign born in the nation as a whole was roughly 8.8 per cent while in California it was more than 13 per cent. The 1930 census for the state lists 368,013 Mexicans. (The 1940 census classes these Mexicans as white.) The 1940 census for the state enumerates 124,306 Negroes, 93,917 Japanese, 39,556 Chinese, 31,408 Filipinos, and 18,675 Indians, while in the city of San Francisco at the same time, out of 634,536 inhabitants, there were 4,846 Negroes, 17,782 Chinese, and 5,846 Japanese. Between 1940 and 1944, the Negro population increased from 4,846 to about 18,000. This increase coincided with the removal of approximately 5,000 Japanese to relocation camps in other parts of the country.[2] The shift in population meant that the community of San Francisco found itself almost overnight in a face-to-face encounter with large groups of Negroes who had come into the state in response to the demands of the war industries. As one acquaintance of mine said to me one day, "I feel squeamish and uneasy when I move around the city now because everywhere I look I see a Negro." And he was a sensitive, educated man of good will. War production forced most industries to hire workers without regard to ethnic or national origin, but on the job and often in the unions themselves there was flagrant discrimination. In housing, residential restrictions sponsored by the Property Owners' Association were operative not only against Oriental and Indian minorities, but also against Negroes. This restriction caused forced and deplorable crowding.

Recreation for nonwhites was inadequate, and understandably. Numerous small Negro churches sprang up, concerned not with

[2] These figures are taken from an unpublished master's thesis, Mills College.

any interracial unraveling but dedicated to giving to these strangers a little island of community. On the other hand, there arose in the community various organizations formed to re-establish some sort of social equilibrium which would make violence and eruptions less likely.

To complete the picture, various headlines from the San Francisco *Chronicle* from September to November, 1943, will give some indication of the general pulse:

Saturday, September 4, 1943
Kenny Calls Sheriff to Race Riot Meeting
Sacramento (AP)—Prevention of race riots was discussed at a meeting of the Sheriffs from nineteen North California counties here today in the office of Attorney General Robert W. Kenny.

Friday, September 10, 1943
Richmond California Has New Race Committee
The Council for American Unity met for the first time last week in Richmond and adopted a four-point program of action to "avert racial disorder." This committee was unofficial unlike the old official committee called the Negroes Tolerance Committee which it is alleged has taken no steps since its formation.

The four point program of the new committee was as follows:

I. To promote equal opportunities for all Americans to participate in the prosecution of the war without discrimination because of race, color, creed or national origin.

II. To promote equal opportunities for all Americans of every race, creed and color to participate in the life of our community and to contribute to its well being.

III. To strengthen the unity of the American people and to make the democratic creed a living reality.

IV. To avert strife and disunity by working together to eliminate racial and religious prejudice from our community life.

The organizations represented were the American Legion, the Lions Club, the NAACP, the YWCA, the Oil Workers Union, the Tolerance Committee, the Bay Area Council Against Discrimination. The nominating committee consisted of two Negroes, two white and two Mexican members.

October 21, 1943
San Francisco May Set Pace in Racial Solution
Charles S. Johnson arrived in the city to conduct a three weeks survey. He feels "a better solution may be arrived at than has been found in large Eastern and Midwestern or Southern cities."

This was the climate in 1944 . . .

1. Khyber Pass

HE WAS THE FIRST person I had ever seen die. I was seven and my father was fifty-five. He had been sick only five days. Late in the afternoon of the fifth day, I stood with my mother beside his bed. His magnificent chest showed the pressure from his lungs, as he fought for air. Up from his throat came the guttural noises which in our community was called the "death rattle." At length my mother said, "Saul, can you hear me?" He nodded his head. Continuing, she said, "Are you ready to die?"

With an effort supreme, he said, "All my life I have been a man, I am not afraid of death, Alice. I can stand it."

At that moment his body was caught in a great spasm that lifted his large frame from the bed. We struggled to hold him down. Suddenly, it was all over. My father was dead.

Because my father had no membership in the local church he was not regarded as a Christian and the minister was unwilling to bury him from the church. In the rooms of our home there was not enough space for the funeral service to be held there. The funeral parlor was available only to white people; even the bodies of Negroes could not be embalmed on the premises of the undertaker's establishment. My grandmother insisted that my father must be buried from the church. She carried her plea to the board of deacons and she received from them the permission to use the sanctuary of the church for the funeral. A traveling evangelist, a Rev. Sam Cromarte, accepted the invitation to conduct the service. This to us was a most gracious act.

During the sermon, to our utter amazement, the minister "preached my father into hell." Here was an object lesson to all unbelievers, to all sinners. As I sat beside my mother on the mourners' seat, I kept saying to her, "He didn't know Poppa? Did he? Did he, Momma?" Tenderly she placed her hands over my bare knees, gently patting them as she whispered comforting and reassuring words to me.

During the long drive from the cemetery I was able to question freely at last. My mother, grandmother, and I talked about what had happened. They tried to explain it to me. Finally I said, "When I grow up to be a man, one thing is sure, I'll never have anything to do with the church."

Nevertheless, owing to the influence of my mother and my grandmother, I grew up in the church sharing deeply in its life.

It was during my second year in high school that I decided to prepare myself for a religious vocation. There was for me a distinct sense of mission in my decision. Strangely enough my decision was rooted in a discovery that I had made which had very little to do with a religious vocation as such. I was a very sensitive child who suffered much from the violences of racial conflict. The climate of our town, Daytona Beach, Florida, was better than most Southern towns because of the influence of the tourists who wintered there. Nevertheless, life became more and more suffocating because of the fear of being brutalized, beaten, or otherwise outraged. In my effort to keep this fear from corroding my life and making me seek relief in shiftlessness, I sought help from God. I found that the more I turned to prayer, to what I discovered in later years to be meditation, the more time I spent alone in the woods or on the beach, the freer became my own spirit and the more realistic became my ambitions to get an education. Here at last was something I could do with my life. But it would call for a different emphasis in the religious life and experience from that which I saw around me in the community.

Perhaps it was the experience of the death of my father and its consequences which gave me an early conditioning against the tendency toward exclusiveness within the Christian church—to be specific, within our local Baptist church. Fortunately for me, the influence of my mother and grandmother tutored me in a kind of Christian experience that was less limiting than the teachings of our particular church. It is difficult to make clear precisely what happened to me during those formative years. Very early I distinguished between the demand to surrender my life to God and thus become a follower of Jesus, on the one hand, and the more prescribed demands of our local church, on the other hand.

Khyber Pass

For instance, when I was "converted" during a children's revival, I came home to tell my mother and grandmother about my experience. I explained that I wanted to learn how to become a Christian. It was the custom that all persons who had been converted must appear before the board of deacons for examination and screening. When my turn came I made my simple statement, only to be told that in order to be accepted for membership in the church, I had to have a Christian experience; and since it seemed to them that I did not have it, I was asked to "go back" until I had such an experience. My grandmother brought me back to the meeting immediately and challenged the deacons with this statement: "How do you know what God is doing in this boy's life? If he cannot join the church so as to learn from other Christians how to be a Christian, where else can he go?" They accepted me.

All through my early years I was in subtle and inarticulate conflict with what seemed to me to be germane to the religious experience of the Christian and what was only a part of the Christian culture, or the Christian etiquette, of our community. The question of the racial exclusiveness of the church was not an issue in my thoughts and feelings during this period for the good reason that the segregated church was taken for granted. I felt that there was no relationship between the white church, for instance, and the Negro church. There was no communication between these two church groups. In my thought there was no distinction in behavior between a white person who belonged to the church and one who did not. In fact, the white people in our town who were most friendly and less antagonistic were numbered principally among those who were not members of any church. Even to this day I find that whenever I see the cross, my mind and my spirit must do a double take, because the thing that flashes instinctively in my mind is that of the burning cross of the Klan.

My decision to go into the Christian ministry came at the end of a period of severe crisis. I could not make clear to any of my friends or my teachers in high school or even to my mother and grandmother the cause of the crisis. As I look back I see that there were three basic elements in it. One, a vague feeling that somehow I was violating my father's memory by taking leadership responsibility in an institution that had done violence to his spirit. Two, the recognition that I could not accept the emphasis upon membership exclusiveness which seemed an authentic part of the genius of the church—the fact that the doctrine of salvation made a gulf between those who belonged to the church as members and those who did not. Three, the examination of the implication of the Christian ministry upon my life and the life around me, caused the question of the segregated church to become an issue—how could I in good conscience accept it? All three of these questions held me back from the acceptance of the call to vocation. On the other hand, there was the clear pull and insistence of the Spirit of God within my own heart, urging me to say Yes to the Light and to trust God with and for the results. At length I found peace in the decision to give my life to the Christian ministry. But always within the shadow of my mind, these three issues kept watch.

By the time that I was a senior in college, the question involving my father's memory was resolved. It was like this. Before the beginning of my senior year I was visiting my family for a few days before the opening of school. One of my boyhood friends took me for a ride around town and showed me the changes that had taken place. We were passing through a part of town called "Midway." It was one of the Negro areas or ghettos. As we drove by a barbershop, I noticed a man standing on the steps. When I saw him, I froze—I turned to Willie Pierce, my friend, saying, "Let's go home. I don't feel well." He thought he had offended me in some way for he was sensitive to the fact that I had gone away to school and he had not. I made it clear that I felt sick and needed to lie down. When I got home, I was telling my grandmother about what had happened. She asked me to describe the man. I did so. Then her face lighted up. "Don't you know who that was, boy? That was Sam Cromarte who preached Saul's funeral."

I was twenty-two years old and I had not seen him since I was seven. In some strange way this experience gave me my release.

My decision to enter the ministry was made despite my deep feeling both about the exclusiveness of the church within the Negro community, and the segregated church in the wider community. At the end of my course at Morehouse College, I was offered an instructorship in economics in my college with an opportunity to go to the University of Chicago to get my B.A.

degree validated; because at that time, 1923, my college was not accredited. This I refused because I wanted to enter a theological seminary. My choice was Newton Theological Institution because many of the persons from the North who visited our high school often referred to it in one way or another. Also, in many of the old church magazines that were sent down to our little library from the North, there were advertisements of this particular school in Massachusetts.

I applied for entrance only to be told in a letter written by the president that Newton did not accept Negroes as students but that I could find the kind of training I needed for religious leadership among *my people* at Virginia Union University, a Negro Baptist school in Richmond, Virginia. (This policy has been changed for many years.)

Thereupon I applied to Rochester Theological Seminary in Rochester, New York, and was told that if my record stood up during my senior year, I would probably be admitted. However, I could not be assured until they were certain that I was the best Negro to apply inasmuch as only one could be accepted. In the very late spring, I received my letter of acceptance. Here at last I was beginning my formal preparation for my vocation. I felt secure in my personal religious commitment in a new way, because I now was definitely on my journey. I was one of two Negroes in the school. My associates, for the first time, were completely outside the Negro world and community. The question of the segregated church began moving from the shadowy places of my mind to a more central place of consideration.

In the first place, all of my fellow students were training to be ministers in white Christian churches. This fact was omnipresent—the points of view in most of my class discussions, the attitudes of the fellows in the bull sessions, the etiquette of the place made this very clear, and this without hostility. Here and there I began to discover fellows who were puzzled by the total situation—fellows who wanted to think and act in school with a freedom which they felt would be denied once they were out. There were some who were determined to free themselves of any racial prejudices with the hope that they would be able to give that same kind of Christian witness in the communities to which they would go.

Two such fellows invited me to be a third man in their suite in a wing of the dormitory. Historically, the Negro students had always occupied two single rooms in the same wing on the theory that they needed to be close to each other for company and reassurance. We talked it over, the two men and I. I moved in. When the administrative officer generally responsible for room assignments was advised, nothing was said directly to me, but my two roommates were put on the carpet for this unusual and in a sense radical departure.

When I was elected president of my class, I was invited into the president's office for felicitation. In the course of his remarks, he said that inasmuch as my people could not stand being completely accepted by white people, he wanted me to exercise great care that this honor which my classmates had bestowed upon me would not go to my head.

It was during this particular year that the superintendent of the building died. He was a very intimate part of the life of the school. The president of the student body invited all the class presidents to be pallbearers at the funeral service which was to be held on the campus. The night before the service Ted, the student body president, came to my room to say that it was the general feeling that if I were one of the pallbearers, it would embarrass the family of the deceased. Therefore, he had to ask me to withdraw.

Slowly, it began to break upon me that within the Christian church, the pattern of segregation was effective without regard particularly to the section of the country in which the church was located. North or South, it made no difference. *This was new to me.* It was then that I was forced to raise the question of the source of authority for the racial exclusiveness of the church. Was the church merely a secular institution in society? Was its behavior a reaction-response to the environment? Was it an adjustment that the church had made contrary to its own religious commitment, or was it fundamental to Christian ethics that racial exclusiveness should be operative? Finally, was there a distinction to be drawn between ethnic exclusiveness and religious-experience exclusiveness? These were some of the questions that were moving around in my mind clamoring for solution as I was preparing myself to enter the Christian ministry.

There was one other important aspect of my basic problem. Where did Jesus of Nazareth and his gospel stand in all of this?

Khyber Pass

Did the church part company with the Master in this particular emphasis on racial exclusiveness or not? In seeking an answer to the question having to do with the life of the Master, I developed the thesis that appears in my book *Jesus and the Disinherited*, which embodied my convictions that the segregated church as such was a reaction response to the environment, and not inherent in the genius of the Christian faith itself. But nowhere in my experience had I ever seen a Christian church that was a living confirmation of my conviction. Deep within me I wondered whether or not my conviction was groundless. Years later my work in organizing The Church for the Fellowship of All Peoples was in its essence an attempt to establish empirical validation for what to me is a profound religious and ethical insight concerning the genius of the church as a religious fellowship. To phrase it in another way, I had to find out for myself whether or not it is true that experiences of spiritual unity and fellowship are more compelling than the fears and dogmas and prejudices that separate men. And if these experiences can be multiplied over a time interval of sufficient duration, would they be able to undermine any barrier that separates one man from another?

The journey from Rochester Theological Seminary to The Church for the Fellowship of All Peoples in San Francisco and later to Marsh Chapel, Boston University, carried me through many experiences, but always the purpose was the same. Religious experience must unite rather than divide men. There must be made available experiences by which the sense of separateness will be transcended and unity expressed, experiences that are deeper than all diversity but at the same time are enriched by diversity.

Following Rochester Seminary my first church was the Mt. Zion Baptist Church in Oberlin, Ohio. After a few weeks as its minister, my congregation began to change its complexion, literally. First, students from the college began attending services, then a few professors, and after a few months some townspeople became regular members of the congregation. In short, for two years my congregation was integrated as far as attendance was concerned, but it is important to point out that during that entire period, not a single white person ever joined the church.

One day my doorbell rang. When I answered I was greeted by a Chinese gentleman who had been attending the services of the church for an entire semester. We had never met. He came to tell me good-by, and to express his appreciation for the experiences of worship which he had in our services. He said, "I am a Buddhist. I did not expect to find a Christian service in which I could worship. This year your church has provided that kind of experience for me and I take back to my country a genuine gratitude for what you have given me." He was the first Buddhist I had ever seen.

Very often delegations of students came from colleges in the general area. One of the groups came periodically from Worcester College and along with them was Mrs. Compton, the mother of the two famous scientists of Washington University and Massachusetts Institute of Technology. I mention these things merely to point out the complexity of the congregation as far as its racial participation in religious services was concerned.

The necessity was laid upon me to address myself to the deepest needs of the human spirit. In order to do this, I had to seek always to discover spiritual insights that moved at a profounder level than the contexts by which these insights were defined. It was like a refining fire to interpret religion each Sunday morning to a congregation which was composed of a few persons who could not read, many of very limited formal education, but also high school, college and seminary students, and a few college professors. In addition to these educational categories, the racial categories were present also, Negro and white, with a few individuals each semester who came from beyond the seas.

After spending two years at Oberlin, one year as a special student of Rufus Jones' at Haverford College, and two and one-half years on the faculty of Morehouse and Spelman Colleges in Atlanta, Georgia, I accepted a position as Professor of Theology and Chairman of the University Committee on Religious Life at Howard University, Washington, D.C. My work at Howard began in the fall of 1932.

In the fall of 1935, I was serving as chairman of a delegation sent on a pilgrimage of friendship undertaken by the students of America to the students of India, Burma, and Ceylon. This trip was the result of a special invitation from the Student Christian Movement of these three countries. These students were accustomed to the thought pattern and religious attitudes of white

American Christians but they felt that there would be a significant inspiration to them to have the shared insights of Negro American Christians. At any rate this was the basis of the invitation. When the invitation was first extended to Mrs. Thurman and me, we declined because it seemed to us to be another expression of segregation within the church. Why a separate Negro delegation? Later when we discovered what the real issue was behind the invitation, we accepted with the provision that we would be free to interpret the Christian religion in accordance with our experience and convictions.

The whole issue of segregation within the church and its resultant inability to challenge the color bar in the present society was presented to us in a sharp and dramatic form within twenty-four hours after our arrival in Colombo, Ceylon, the starting point for our pilgrimage.

I was invited to give a talk before the Law College at the University at Ceylon. The assigned subject was Civil Disabilities under States' Rights in the United States. At the close of the talk and the question period, I was invited to coffee by the principal. We drank our coffee in silence. After the service had been removed, he said to me, "What are you doing over here? I know what the newspapers say about a pilgrimage of friendship and the rest, but that is not my question. What are *you* doing over here? This is what I mean. More than three hundred years ago your forefathers were taken from the western coast of Africa as slaves. The people who dealt in the slave traffic were Christians. One of your famous Christian hymn writers, Sir John Newton, made his money from the sale of slaves to the New World. He is the man who wrote 'How Sweet the Name of Jesus Sounds' and 'Glorious Things of Thee Are Spoken'—there may be others, but these are the only ones I know. The name of one of the famous British slave vessels was *Jesus*.

"The men who bought slaves were Christians. Christian ministers, quoting the Christian apostle Paul, gave the sanction of religion to the system of slavery. Some seventy years or more ago you American Negroes were freed by a man who was not a professing Christian, but was rather the spearhead of certain political, social, and economic forces, the significance of which he himself did not understand. During all the period since then you have lived in a Christian nation in which you are segregated, lynched, and burned. Even in the church, I understand, there is segregation. One of my students who went to your country to study sent me a clipping telling about a Christian church in which the regular Sunday worship was interrupted so that many could join a mob against one of your fellows. When he had been caught and done to death, they came back to resume their worship of their Christian God.

"I am a Hindu. I do not understand. Here you are in my country, standing deep within the Christian faith and tradition. I do not wish to seem rude to you, but sir, I think you are a traitor to all the darker peoples of the earth. I am wondering what you, an intelligent man, can say in defense of your position."

In almost every city we visited, in varied ways the same question was raised—why is the church powerless before the color bar? All answers had to be defensive because there was not a *single instance* known to me in which a local church had a completely integrated membership. The color bar was honored in the practice of the Christian religion. From a 10,000-mile perspective, this monumental betrayal of the Christian ethic loomed large and forbidding.

Near the end of our journey we spent a day in Khyber Pass on the border of the northwest frontier. It was an experience of vision. We stood looking at a distance into Afghanistan, while to our right, and close at hand, passed a long camel train bringing goods and ideas to the bazaars of North India. Here was the gateway through which Roman and Mogul conquerors had come in other days bringing with them goods, new concepts, and the violence of armed might. All that we had seen and felt in India seemed to be brought miraculously into focus. We saw clearly what we must do somehow when we returned to America. We knew that we must test whether a religious fellowship could be developed in America that was capable of cutting across all racial barriers, with a carry-over into the common life, a fellowship that would alter the behavior patterns of those involved. It became imperative now to find out if experiences of spiritual unity among people could be more compelling than the experiences which divide them.

At Howard University I began experimenting at once with

forms of worship other than those to be found in a regular religious service with the sermon as the pivotal point. Even within the regular service I provided an increasingly large place for meditation, quiet, and the prayer experiences which resulted therefrom. But this was but the beginning. Could worship experience through the fine arts, for instance, provide a unity among people that would be compelling? Several experiments were conducted. The simplest vehicle would be a vesper service because there was more freedom at that time than in the conventional Sunday morning service. We called the vesper services "Twilight Hours." This was a convenient encompassing title that announced the fact but gave little aid to any preconceived notion.

Among the various "Twilight Hours" which we developed three will find a place here. There was a felt need for giving to the university community with its great diversity in religious backgrounds, though well-nigh complete homogeneity as to race, a feel of and for the majesty and vitality of the Bible. I thought that if I could make a comprehensive selection of great passages which told the story of man's quest for God, this would give to all who shared them a sense of unity in heritage and in quest. I used both the Old and New Testaments, finding the passages that dealt sometimes dramatically, sometimes rebelliously, sometimes redemptively or devotionally with the basic theme. These selections were mimeographed as one connected story. What was the content of such vesper service? There was a meditative organ prelude, at the end of which I introduced the idea behind the selections. Then for one hour I read the material aloud with the organ weaving in and out a muted accompaniment with long breaths of silence here and there. When the service was over I left the pulpit—the audience remained in silence for a full five minutes before anyone moved. As they went out the ushers gave to each a copy of what had been read.

The most daring of the "Twilight Hours" was the introduction of the dance as an experience of spiritual unity. This was most hazardous because of the general attitude toward the dance as such—plus the fact that many of our community had had no previous exposure to so-called aesthetic dancing. I met, through Mrs. Thurman, a young Roman Catholic dancer who lived in Baltimore. She had a vital interest in recapturing the dance as an act of Christian worship. I selected four of the universal moods of the human spirit that were present wherever men worshiped their God: Praise—Thanksgiving—Contrition—Faith. Appropriate readings were found, some of them biblical (this was most important). A careful selection of music was made by the dancer in co-operation with the chapel organist. The choreography was designed for a solo dancer.

I prepared the community for the service by a series of systematic announcements with comments in the Sunday bulletin and by discussing the idea with all and sundry in my daily contacts around the campus. At first, sport was made of the idea with many cynical remarks. I had to insist that the dancer wear flowing robes.

At last the day arrived. The chapel was packed. I could sense the curious mixture of anticipation, skepticism, and honest inquiry and seeking. The organist opened the service with a prelude, after which I read passages concerning Praise—the dancer entered and the moment was hers. It was like the waiting seconds just before the sun appears above the horizon at day's dawning—would the sunlight appear or would it be hidden behind mist and cloud? It was as if a wall was removed and we became one people, feeling one thing. It was magnificent. The rest followed in tempo and quality.

Here was a young white woman, a Roman Catholic by religious faith, sharing an experience of profoundest spiritual significance with a group made up largely of Negroes, in a religious service, Protestant Christian in orientation. What happened there was authentic in and of itself. It was *an experience of* convincement!

Perhaps the most dramatic of the "Twilight Hours" and one which, for nearly ten years, became a chapel tradition was Living Madonnas with Ave Marias. I made a careful study of as many madonnas as I could find in museums and particularly in color reproductions of Italian paintings. Then I made a selection of five, copies of which were available in small reproductions. The idea was to render a life-size reproduction of a particular painting, giving careful attention to details of costume, pose, and colors. I talked it over with a teacher of painting and the director of the university's art gallery. At first the idea seemed impractical and even if it were not, what was the point? I thought that if we could have a Twilight Hour during which, at intervals of eight to ten minutes, each picture was reproduced with a living subject under appropriate lighting, the congregation could experience the beauty and the spiritual quality of the painting independent of the fact that the painting itself came out of a particular tradition within Christianity. But something was lacking in the feeling of the idea. Could it be communicated in this single dimension? Then the thought came that if, while the pose was being held, an Ave Maria was played or sung, this would help to assure communication. The school of music became involved at this point.

I needed a skilled person to help with the costuming. The Home Economics Department provided such a person. A carpenter built a large picture frame about 9 by 5 feet. Across it was stretched theatrical gauze. It was placed in the center of the platform in the chapel. Lights were arranged so that illumination could be from the top, the bottom, and the sides of the frame. Velvet curtains were hung from the wall on either side. Into this frame the painting was reproduced. The interior of the frame was dark while the pose was arranged. Then slowly the lights came up giving full illumination; simultaneously, the music of the Ave Maria was heard. The effect was that of a mild electric current shooting through the congregation. In the interval between each reproduction, there was the long silence. It was what Otto calls "the numinous silence of waiting."

During the early fall I would study many faces and observe many students, both girls and boys. The casting was done in my own mind without consultation. When the decision was made, I would talk with the individuals inviting them to participate. To each was given a color reproduction of the particular painting. The request was made that this picture be placed so that it could be seen daily at close range. There was one dress rehearsal, but several meetings to work on the matter of the pose and the costuming. More than one girl attested to the fact that living daily with the picture and participating in the service itself had wrought far-reaching changes in the meaning of religious experience. It is of interest to add that I had one real artistic advantage over the original artist—the colors of my models ranged from albino white to burnt umber. This made for a symphonic arrangement that was extraordinary.

These three experiments and others like them with Worship through the Fine Arts gave me more important confirmation of the fact that a way could be found to unite people of great ideological and religious diversity through experiences which were more compelling than the concepts that separated and divided. Even though the environment was somewhat controlled and to that extent artificial, the faith in the creative possibilities of such experience could not be devalued.

2. In This Commitment

IT WAS AGAINST this background that I received a fateful letter from A. J. Muste of the Fellowship of Reconciliation. It was the fall of 1943. But behind this letter is the story of the restiveness of a small group of people in San Francisco who could no longer abide the narrow boundaries of their religious upbringing and who were particularly challenged by the phenomenal increase in the Negro population owing to the importation of workers to meet the increasing demands of total war.

The central moving figure among this group was Dr. Alfred G. Fisk, a Presbyterian clergyman who was a professor of philosophy at the San Francisco State College. He took the initiative, not in his capacity as a college professor nor even as a Presbyterian clergyman, but rather because he was a human being of acute sensitivity with a deep desire to extend the experience of brotherhood to all people. As a clergyman of the Presbyterian Church, U.S.A., he had a vocational vehicle which could be useful in an attempt to formalize his undertaking.

Gathered around him was a nucleus of young adults familiarly designated as the "Sakai" group, so called because most of them lived co-operatively in a house owned by the Sakai family, all of whom had been removed from the area during the involuntary withdrawal of Japanese-Americans from the Pacific coast. This group had been deeply influenced toward the simple life by Miss Muriel Lester. They wanted to live in the midst of the densely populated Negro area brought into being by war demands on industry. They sought to share a common life among these Negroes and to help them with their individual and collective needs. In addition to the "Sakais," there were others who were acutely conscious of injustice and who were glad to share in the simple but dramatic witness of brotherhood practiced in common worship. The group was small and yet diversified. In this group there were young people with skills and talents which were a part of their offering. One young lady was a gifted pianist, a graduate of Mt. Holyoke College. It was she who provided the music for all occasions. There were others who typed expertly which made possible mimeographed programs for the Sunday service. One person who always regarded herself as without special talents became the janitress. She took great delight in keeping the meeting place clean and arranged the simple furniture to communicate "We are glad you have come." Often she went around the neighborhood gathering little children about her for stories and for games. Coming upon her at such a time, one could sense a radiance even if eyes were too dull to see it.

The need the group felt was for the kind of fellowship that would involve the immediate neighborhood. Such a fellowship would be an oasis in a rather blighted area. There was no thought of doing more than this. Even such an undertaking demanded high courage and special daring. The first tentative name chosen was "The Neighborhood Church." Note, please, that there was no creedal or polity basis for their unity in worship. There was no organizational structure.

Dr. Fisk guided the group in regular worship services on Sunday mornings. He was able to interest the Presbyterian denomination through its local representative. With special funds, the Presbyterians made available a place for worship and for the simplest neighborhood activities, and provided money with which to pay, in part, the salaries of professional workers. Dr. Fisk could give only part of his time to this development because he continued as a full-time professor in the State College, but he was able to secure the services of Manley Johnson, a young Negro theological student, to help in the work of the fellowship.

During this period the activities were simple and limited. There was a Sunday morning worship service led by the two ministers; there was an occasional pot-luck supper to which many more people came than were ever present in the worship services. There was a small Sunday School made up largely of children from the immediate neighborhood.

While the group was hoping to find someone who could give all of his time to the permanent establishment of a neighborhood church founded on this conception, Dr. Fisk took the initiative by writing to several people across the United States for suggestions that might help to secure a young Negro just out of seminary who would be willing to come to California and devote all his time to the fellowship. One of the persons to whom Dr. Fisk wrote was A. J. Muste.

Mr. Muste referred Dr. Fisk's letter to me on the assumption that I would know about the availability of such a person. At first there was no "pick up" either in my mind or imagination. I saw no connection between this "stirring" in San Francisco and the quest upon which I had been engaged for so long a time.

I wrote Dr. Fisk, giving him the name of a young man who in my judgment would be an ideal choice. Dr. Fisk wrote to him only to discover that he was not interested. It seemed impractical and completely without challenge. Again, Dr. Fisk wrote to me for further suggestions, expressing his very great concern that someone be found. It was now for the first time that there was kindled in my mind the *possibility* that this may be *the* opportunity toward which my life had been moving. The conception was limited but I thought I saw in it the germ of the great possibility. I told Dr. Fisk that I was interested in joining them and would seek a leave of absence from my post at Howard University. If this could be accomplished, Mrs. Thurman and I would come to San Francisco.

The more we discussed the possibility, the more we felt the pull. San Francisco with its varied nationalities, its rich intercultural heritages, and its face resolutely fixed toward the Orient at a moment when the fate of America hung in the balance from Guam to Yokohama—San Francisco was the ideal center.

In 1943, I applied to the trustees of Howard University for a year's leave of absence, to become effective July 1, 1944. In a fateful conference with the president I told him in detail what I wanted to do and why. He listened with mounting interest. I knew that what I had in mind was something about which, for many years, his was a prophetic voice: indicting the Christian church because of its practice of segregation.

At length he said, "You are not due for a sabbatical for some time. The university cannot make any of your salary available to you. How on earth can you support your family on two hundred dollars a month? How will you manage? How will you live?"

My answer was direct and unself-conscious: "I don't know. All I know is, God will take care of us."

It had been our family custom for many years to arrive at all decisions which affected us as a unit by a democratic device which we called the "House Meeting." Our older daughter was at the Northfield School for Girls in Massachusetts. On a certain weekend when I was scheduled to preach at Smith College, Mrs. Thurman, our younger daughter, and I spent the first part of the weekend at the Northfield Inn. This made possible a special House Meeting to consider the California plan. I explained in detail what it was all about, how their mother and I had felt the need for doing something like this ever since our experience in India. Very carefully I interpreted for each daughter what it would mean: a radical alteration of our way of life, its living conditions, its opportunities, its amenities. That certain privations were inevitable was made abundantly clear. After more than two hours of discussion the time came for the vote.

Since I was presiding I asked that each person should give the reason for his vote. Our younger daughter was the last to cast her vote. Instead of saying Yes or No, she sprang up from her chair, exclaiming, "Hurray for the leave of absence. California, here we come!"

There was much publicity given the fact that we were leaving Washington to attempt something new in American Christianity. The local Council of Churches organized a citizens' committee, under the leadership of Coleman Jennings, a lay reader in the Episcopal Church and a personal friend of many years, to plan a testimonial. A dinner was held in the Universalist Church, one of the few places in which a "mixed group" could meet in those years, for such an occasion. The major address was given by Mrs. Franklin D. Roosevelt and a Godspeed statement by Dr. Mordecai Johnson, the president of Howard University.

Mrs. Roosevelt had been interested in our plan for this work since the middle of the winter. A friend of hers in New York City who gave me the first contribution toward the Children's Intercultural Workshop of the church suggested that I tell Mrs. Roosevelt about my dream and the adventure. When I saw her she was most gracious and gave to me the kind of encouragement that is so expressive of her amazing gift of intimacy.

The group in San Francisco was informed of our coming early in the year but no formal announcement could be made until after the regular board meeting of the trustees of Howard University in April. As soon as Dr. Fisk received final assurance, he and I through regular correspondence worked together on all the plans which we continued upon my arrival in San Francisco. The fact that I was willing to leave the East and my established position there to cast my lot with this small unorganized but faithful group of people committed to this undertaking, gave them heart and courage to hold fast to their venture which in turn heartened and encouraged me. When the announcement was made public, I received letters from friends in the San Francisco Bay Area expressing a real interest in the new undertaking. Many friends in the East rallied to the dream and its possibilities. There were others who were skeptical of this decision and thought I was sick in mind.

During the interval between my agreement to come and the beginning of my leave from the university, Dr. Fisk and I agreed to invite a young Negro clergyman, Albert Cleage, from the East who was available for the six-month period ending July 1, 1944. He was recommended by the late Dr. Charles S. Johnson, of Fisk University, who had spent some time in San Francisco making one of the community surveys for which he was internationally known. Mrs. Thurman, our daughters, and I arrived in San Francisco in July, 1944.

The Board of National Missions of the Presbyterian Church was deeply interested in this turn of events. They agreed to underwrite the venture to the amount of $3600 per year—$2400 for my salary and $1200 for Dr. Fisk's—and to place at our disposal property they owned at 1500 Post Street in which there was a small chapel on the first floor and living quarters—our first home in San Francisco—on the second floor. The building had formerly housed the Japanese-American Presbyterian Church.

Upon our arrival we found in the fellowship a small but eager group numbering fewer than fifty persons. There was no formal organization. A steering committee for the group was designated as a temporary board of which the ministers served as acting chairmen. The group was made up of individuals who offered a variety of specific religious backgrounds: Presbyterians, Baptists, Methodists, Episcopalians, Congregationalists, and a margin of people who had never had any formal religious affiliation. They represented various elements of the immediate community—public school teachers, skilled and unskilled laborers, social workers, businessmen, nurses, housewives. The age distribution ranged from the early twenties to the late fifties.

Our first community-wide activity was a day camp for children, conducted during July and August of 1944 at 1500 Post Street. The children were recruited from the public schools in the immediate neighborhood. Funds to finance this undertaking were granted by the Rosenberg Foundation of San Francisco; a local labor union provided the cost of a daily lunch prepared by a committee of women from a local church. At first the summer camp was run like a Daily Vacation Bible School. However, we soon realized that the plan should be more comprehensive and inclusive; it was this broader conception that interested the Rosenberg Foundation—namely, that children enjoy the unity of fellowship because they are not separated by background or racial or religious prejudices.

An interesting feature of this initial summer camp program was the co-directorship by two young women: Jacqueline Myles, Negro, from the East, an alumna of Bennett College and a graduate student in social work; and from the West, Heather Whitton, white, a graduate student in religious education at the San Francisco Theological Seminary.

The theme of the camp and its program were built around what was termed "Adventures in Friendship," the purpose being to deepen the interest of the children in other peoples and other races, to feed this interest with factual materials, and to let the children experience the art, music, and artifacts of other cultures—American Indian, Mexican, Filipino, Russian, Japanese, Chinese, and Jewish. The program included songs, stories, handcrafts, worship materials, and games from those cultures.

Visiting nationals of the groups under study added much to our appreciation of people other than ourselves. When Father Palmajar, Filipino Episcopal rector, visited the summer camp, the children could not help loving his kindly gracious manner. They were fascinated by the floral tapestry and the beautiful dress woven from pineapple fiber he had brought. Nor would they forget when he showed them how the Filipino women sang as they worked.

We tried always to present all other peoples as real persons, much like ourselves. We wanted the children to think of the American Indians, for instance, as contemporary citizens of our country, and so we arranged for a lovely Indian girl, a cadet nurse in a city hospital, to visit our camp and tell us how she grew up and went to school—we knew it was very much like our own experiences. It was difficult for the children to believe that she was a "real" Indian, dressed as she was in her attractive cadet nurse uniform. One child asked her, "Do you eat acorns?" Those children will never forget that Indians today are "just like other people."

How little the children knew of the culture of other people was surprising. Our excursion to Chinatown, for instance, was the first visit to that section for many of them. It was an exciting experience for them to see the Chinese Post Office and Telephone Exchange, and to watch a group of men reading a Chinese newspaper glued to a wall. Seeing the statue of Sun Yat-sen recalled to them this "George Washington" of China we had told them about, and they recognized in the shops and on the lamp posts the dragons and other Chinese symbols they had studied in camp.

We "made friends" with some Russian children who were pictured on a big Russian poster and learned about the kind of life they were leading during World War II. Our children found in the poster, children of various nationality types. "He looks like me," said a Filipino boy—and a Negro and white boy found themselves, too. They hoped that one day children all over the world would understand one another and be friends.

When we took up the study of Americans of Japanese descent, we began by saying that we were in a building which had been formerly used by them as a church, and that many in the community were living in houses in which the Japanese had lived. We had many beautiful objects of Japanese art which fascinated the children. We told them how the Japanese on the West Coast had been sent away from their community because of the war and how sad they were to leave their homes and friends and go to relocation camps. We distinguished carefully between the Japanese war makers and the people of our community who were loyal Americans of Japanese descent. When at the end of the summer the children wrote their reactions to what the summer had meant to them, one child of ten said: "I will be glad when the Japanese come back to San Francisco so that I may know and learn even more about them."

When the turn came to study the American Negro, we began by telling of Crispus Attucks, a Negro, and the first American to fall in the Boston Massacre. There followed Booker T. Washington and George Washington Carver; also Harriet Tubman, a Union spy during the Civil War who was one of the organizers and conductors of the Underground Railroad; we told of Miss Jane Bolin, the first Negro woman to be appointed justice of a domestic court in New York; and of Mrs. Mary McLeod Bethune, a great contemporary American who with only one dollar and fifty cents and a magnificent dream founded Bethune-Cookman College. And of course, we sang Negro spirituals—and explained the background which gave them birth.

The study of the Jewish people was begun with the simple statement that Jesus was a Jew, and that most of the Bible was written by Jews—statements which the children found at first bewildering because they had not consciously thought of the Jewish people as having given the world so much of its religious heritage. We told them about Albert Einstein and his contributions, of Yehudi Menuhin, a native Californian, and of Fritz Kreisler. The story of Lillian Wald and her Henry Street Settlement House was most exciting to them. *Porgy and Bess* was just then being announced for a future San Francisco showing, so we took occasion to point to the genius of George Gershwin and the musical drama's blending of Negro and Jewish cultures.

Our effort was always to elicit an appreciative response. In discussing the wonderful arts and handcrafts of the Mexicans, we illustrated them with objects which delighted the children. For instance, there was a glazed pottery pig with gay flowers across its back. Before showing it we asked the children what they considered the dirtiest of all animals, and they knew: a pig. Then we showed them the pottery pig. "Must not a people who can make such a beautiful object out of such a dirty animal have a very wonderful sense of beauty?" we asked. And we saw how our little Mexican boys glowed!

The camp was never a time of "study"; it was not like a "school" program; it was a time of play and fun. Frequent excursions were made to San Francisco parks, beaches, ethnic churches, museums, and local centers of various cultures. The children were divided into two age groups so that the program and activities would suit them. The boys did some very fine woodwork; the older girls some nice sewing. One of the most notable activities which attracted city-wide attention was the original paintings of "international subjects" conducted by a gifted young artist, Dianne Daynish, who managed to enlist the interest and creativity of the children in a remarkable fashion. That fall the De Young Museum exhibited a group of the children's watercolors.

In the work of the adult group it was immediately clear that certain fundamental principles must be brought into focus and applied to purpose, goals, and commitment. From the beginning I knew that the neighborhood basis of the group had to be replaced by a broader and more comprehensive concept. True, there were a few people, primarily those in the leadership, who did not live in the neighborhood but that did not alter the local neighborhood concept on the basis of which the group had come together. All of my thinking and experimenting for more than a dozen years had revolved around a much larger and more comprehensive concept. Now I was faced with the specific demand to make a formulation that would provide the religious basis for spiritual experiences of unity among a group of this heterogeneity. I tried to find a way to provide, to create, a religious commitment revealing the profound desire for community which would at the same time give room enough for honoring particular religious backgrounds in the lives of the people entering into the fellowship.

I talked the matter over with various members of the acting board. The general reaction was—"Don't do it. If you do, you will splinter the group. No one would be satisfied. So long as you do not write anything out then there will be no problem. Besides, in matters of religious belief we are likely to be as far apart as we are together in what we are doing."

Nevertheless it seemed to me that if we did not have some kind of verbal platform upon which to stand all authentic growth would be cut off. Day and night I wrestled with the problem—putting at the disposal of it my meditation, my prayers, and as much of a disciplined mind as I possessed. After many writings and rewritings the following commitment was born:

I desire to have a part in the unfolding of the ideal of Christian fellowship through the union of men and women of varying national, cultural, and racial heritage, in church communion.

In this commitment I am pledged to the growing understanding of all men as sons of God and seek after a vital interpretation of the highest manifestation of God—Jesus Christ—in all my relationships.

I desire the strength of corporate worship with the imperative of personal dedication which will be found through membership in the Fellowship Church of San Francisco.[1]

Before presenting it to the board, Dr. Fisk and I talked many hours concerning the words and their implication. At his suggestion we discussed it with the executive secretary of the San Francisco Council of Churches, Dr. Hughbert H. Landram, a friend of the movement. I had worked with him at an early period when he was the West Coast Student Secretary for the YMCA. I thought it advisable to discuss it with a few concerned laymen in the fellowship.

At last the time came for presenting the statement to the board. Dr. Fisk presided and introduced the need for some kind of formal commitment. Every person spoke to the issue. Many questions were asked: Is this to be a creed to which we must subscribe? Is this a profession of our religious faith? One person raised a question about the reference to Jesus Christ as the highest manifestation of God—someone else thought that the reference to Jesus was not sufficient—it was too vague. It was good to talk—healthy, serious, devoted talk.

The statement was accepted on the conviction that it should be used as a working paper for the group. It was to be our commitment of intent, an immediate platform upon which to stand before the community and the world but not a ceiling either for our hopes or our achievement. With this agreement within the board we were ready now to consider communicating this as a recommendation to the little congregation. Remember that there was no organic relatedness within the weekly congregation. We were a fellowship, a very loose fellowship at that. We were on the defensive before the Christian community because we were without status. In some minds we were just a bit up the ladder from the storefront churches that had begun springing up all over the area. The one saving grace was the fact that apparently self-respecting white people were always in attendance.

[1] See pages 52 and 158 for later restatements of the Commitment.

How does one propose something about which there must be a sense of unanimity before it can be accepted? The essence of communication involves identical agendas. Otherwise there can be no communication among individuals or groups. How to get this commitment on the agenda of the individuals making up the fellowship was a tough question to work out.

While the board was discussing the whole idea an exciting notion leaped into my mind. Why not divide the commitment up into phrases or sections and preach a series of Sunday morning sermons on them? But this would not be practical unless I could have a series of Sunday mornings during which I preached each sermon. The current arrangement was that Dr. Fisk and I would preach on alternate Sundays. It was necessary to approach the matter of equality from the outside even as we were trying to develop the feel for it within. It went so far at first that it was a part of the etiquette for us to sing out of the same hymnal—it was a symbol of equality between the Negro and the white man. Unless one has walked all the way through the beginnings of what we were undertaking, such a symbol may seem quite childish.

I proposed that inasmuch as Dr. Fisk was taking his vacation in Mexico and would be away during the month of August, I should do all the preaching. It was not necessary to invite a white minister to preach on Dr. Fisk's Sundays. The plan was accepted enthusiastically.

I preached the series of sermons on the commitment. This meant that the group itself had the opportunity to experience a growing understanding of the commitment through thinking together about its meaning in an atmosphere of worship. During this period there was much informal discussion about the ideas. There began to emerge a thought-out sense of togetherness and a hard core of purpose around which all of our participation and our living could be integrated. At the end of the period an invitation was extended to the congregation to sign such a commitment as an expression of formal affiliation.

As a result of having shared in a "fellowship of understanding," prior to formal affiliation, there came into being, for the first time, this group of people now related to one another in ways symbolized by this signed commitment. This was the initial step in the formal organization of The Church for The Fellowship of All Peoples. Thus ended the first phase of the mission that had brought us three thousand miles across the continent to San Francisco.

It seemed wise at this juncture to hold a service of formal recognition of the church to which the city of San Francisco could be invited. This occasion was conceived as an official launching of the church as a going concern. It was possible now because there was an actual membership. As the plans for this public inaugural service developed, the idea became more and more compelling. There were, however, three problems. Where could such a meeting be held? What kind of program would enlist the imagination and the concern of the varied segments of the community? How could we interest the news media of the city in the formal launching of a church?

Here I must recount dramatic evidence of the movement of the finger of God in our undertaking, abundant manifestations of which emerged through the years. When Mrs. Thurman and I were journeying from the East to California, we were able to get Pullman accommodations only as far as Salt Lake City, because of the wartime travel difficulties. At Salt Lake City a single upper was available. Just before the train pulled out of the railway station, I had a casual conversation with a fellow passenger who had discovered that we too were en route to San Francisco. I found that he and his wife were returning to their home from a vacation. He very graciously gave us one of the two sections they had secured. Later during the journey I told him about our mission to San Francisco and the dream of the enterprise as I felt and sensed it. It developed that he was Winthrop Martin, a public relations expert who served as volunteer publicity chairman for the newly created San Francisco Council of Churches. He also had a radio program on Saturday afternoons. When we separated, he said, "If there is anything I can do to help you launch the idea in the city when the times comes, please call on me."

Hence, I now turned to him with the plans for the formal inaugural service of the church. He worked wonders. He got the local newspapers to give the coming event wide coverage. He arranged a special radio interview on the Saturday before the inaugural service, between the comptroller of San Francisco, a widely honored and respected man in the community and incidentally a Roman Catholic, and myself. He made sure that newspaper reporters and news photographers from all the dailies would be present at the service. The publicity for this important event could hardly have been better.

For officiating participants we turned naturally to the one denomination that had been involved in the development of the neighborhood church idea from the beginning—the Presbyterian Church. We wanted to have our initial meeting in one of the local Presbyterian churches, but this idea proved embarrassing. So we sought and were given the hearty co-operation of the First Unitarian Church in San Francisco and accordingly, our inaugural service was held in that sanctuary on Sunday afternoon, October 8, 1944.

In planning the program for the occasion it was important to call attention to the new dimension in which we would be venturing from the formal opening forward. Particularly was I concerned that, in every possible detail, even the afternoon's activities would yield one basic unifying experience that would temporarily transcend all the barriers of religion and culture and race. The presiding officer was Dr. Ezra Allen Van Nuys, representing the Presbytery of San Francisco. The invocation was given by the Rt. Rev. Edward L. Parsons, retired Bishop of Grace Cathedral of San Francisco. Bishop Parsons was chairman of the board of the local chapter of the American Civil Liberties Union. In his person and life he held a unique place in the city as a clergyman who stood in a clear spot against bigotry wherever it manifested itself, even in the church. This he did without ever seeming in any sense to be less a profound and devoted Christian. Greetings were brought from Rev. John C. Leffler, president of the San Francisco Council of Churches; Rev. F. D. Haynes, president of the Ministerial Alliance, an organization of Negro clergymen; Rabbi Elliot M. Burstein, chairman, the Northern California Board of Rabbis and Cantors; and Rev. Buell G. Gallagher, co-pastor, the South Berkeley Community Church.

Dr. Fisk made a statement about the neighborhood beginnings and under what necessity he felt to share in an experience like ours. He spoke from the topic "A Venture in Christian Fellowship." I gave the major address of the afternoon in which, using the theme, "A Vital Religion in the Modern World," I stated my own convictions about the unifying power of religion which need not violate the contexts of meanings by which religion, in particular instances, may be defined. In essence it was a confession of my religious faith and the kind of demand which it laid upon me.

The Prayer of Dedication was given by Rev. Ralph Marshall Davis, minister, the First Presbyterian Church of Oakland. He was a man of rare mystical insights who in his religious experience seemed to me to have been untrammeled by forms and institutions. The Benediction was given by Rev. C. F. F. Dutton, minister, the First Unitarian Church. The hymns were chosen most carefully. They were two. At the beginning the large congregation lifted itself up on wings of aspiration:

> O God, our help in ages past,
>   Our hope for years to come,
> Our shelter from the stormy blast,
>   And our eternal home.
>
> Before the hills in order stood,
>   Or earth received her frame,
> From everlasting Thou art God,
>   To endless years the same.
>
> A thousand ages in Thy sight
>   Are like an evening gone;
> Short as the watch that ends the night
>   Before the rising sun.
>
> Time, like an ever-rolling stream,
>   Bears all its sons away;
> They fly forgotten, as a dream
>   Dies at the opening day.
>
> Our God, our help in ages past;
>   Our hope for years to come;
> Be Thou our guide while troubles last,
>   And our eternal home!

At the end there was the hymn of longing, of frustration, and of hope:

> When wilt Thou save the people?
> O God of mercy, when?
> Not kings and lords, but nations!
> Not thrones and crowns, but men!

Flowers of Thy heart, O God, are they;
Let them not pass, like weeds, away—
Their heritage, a sunless day.
   God save the people!

Shall crime bring crime forever,
   Strength aiding still the strong?
Is it Thy will, O Father,
   That man shall toil for wrong?
'No,' say Thy mountains; 'No,' Thy skies;
Man's clouded sun shall brightly rise,
And songs ascend, instead of sighs.
   God save the people!

When wilt Thou save the people?
   O God of mercy, when?
The people, Lord, the people,
   Not thrones and crowns, but men!
God save the people; Thine they are,
Thy children as Thine angels fair;
From vice, oppression, and despair,
   God save the people!

   It was a kind of prophetic fulfillment to hold our service at the First Unitarian Church. This was, after all, a fitting place because of the historic contribution that this church, through one of its former ministers, Thomas Starr King, had made to the struggle to liberate the slaves during the fateful years when the House was divided. King's tremendous powers were in no small measure responsible for California's strategic contribution to the Union's cause and to human freedom.

   Immediately we were faced with two problems created somewhat by the effect of our service of inauguration. One was the temptation to despair as a reaction to the contrast between the vast possibilities of our undertaking and the simple fact that we were a little group without organization, holding our services in a small chapel that had been converted from a living room in an ordinary dwelling house. The distance between the fact and the image was such that only God could span. The second problem had to do with the necessity for moving out of our present location into a place which would provide for growth in members and program.

   If we moved it would have to be out of the Fillmore area. This would take us away from the section in which there was the largest percentage of Negroes. Thus it would destroy the reason for being that called the original group into existence. If our aim was to provide a friendly place of worship for Negroes and those other persons not Negroes who wished to share in our fellowship, then to move out of the area would be a denial of our intent.

I was aware of this. I knew also that religious institutions all over America had been made agents of segregation by virtue of their location in segregated neighborhoods. It does not matter what the intent and the purpose of an institution is in its dedication to brotherhood, if it is in a geographically segregated district, and if it accepts as its assignment the meeting of the needs of the people in that district, such an institution in time will become like the district—segregated. In the light of this fact I knew that if we did not move, we would become a Negro church in a comparatively short time or disappear entirely.

The issue had to be met head on. A combined meeting of the congregation and the board was called to work out a solution. It was a long meeting with heated discussion. There was almost unanimous resistance to the idea. The resistance was understandable and for it I had great understanding. The argument ran something like this: if we move out of the district, it will mean that we are running away from the social problem of separateness, that we are declaring that as a church we are above the struggle and therefore cannot be depended upon to contribute anything directly to (encourage) the self-respect of people who were ghetto-bound. This attitude within the congregation was strengthened by a general feeling that although I was a Negro, I had come to San Francisco directly out of the atmosphere of an American university and therefore should be expected to have ivory-tower notions. Further, that with my training and experience I was out of sympathy with the plight and the predicament of the masses of my fellows. The argument continued that the church belonged in the midst of the greatest need and was there to do its perfect work on behalf of the Kingdom of God.

It was in vain for me to deny the judgment that was being leveled against me because it could not be met by argument. I insisted, however, that if the church remained in the Fillmore district and developed as a neighborhood church, in an incredibly short time it would become a Negro church. In my judgment this would merely herald the appearance in San Francisco of one more segregated religious institution, and I would have no sympathy for this basic denial of the true meaning of the gospel of God. A combined meeting of the congregation and the board, called to decide the issue, finally brought it to a head. Everyone there recongized the risks if we moved. Everyone saw clearly our fate if we did not move. Too many could not decide. As I look back upon the meeting the turning point came when I told the group the following story:

A friend of mine wrote me a letter telling how wild crab apples grow in one of the New England states. She said that first one tiny shoot comes up and as quickly as it develops to a certain height, the deer eat the tender leaves and the plant dies. Other shoots come up with the same result, until at last there is a rather thickly matted area of thorny vestigial remains of former plants whose tiny bruised trunks have dried and sharpened under the rays of the sun and the ministry of the wind. Now at last in the center of this area a shoot comes up which eventually becomes a matured fruit tree because when the deer try to get to it again, the tender parts of their hoofs are pierced by the sharp stalks. When the shoot is big enough so that the deer can stand on the edge of the area and eat the leaves, it is then strong enough to stand whatever the deer can do to it. I said to the congregation, "Let's move out of this district until the character of our undertaking is sufficiently rooted in us and in the community. When that time comes it will not matter where in San Francisco the church is located. It will be able to withstand whatever relentless social pressures may be brought to bear upon it by the total community." We decided to move and fortunately this decision was facilitated by the fact that after our inaugural service the number of people who began attending our church was greater than our chapel could accommodate. Thus we could move with everybody's face saved and the fundamental genius of the undertaking left intact.

Finding another meeting house in a more inclusive community was not easy because of the demands for space of all kinds created by the war effort in San Francisco in 1944. In the general area but out of the ghetto section were two club houses with auditoriums. These large rooms were available for a fee. We found that the time which we required for Sunday services was free in both places. The manager of one these club houses was called to see if we could rent the space regularly and at what cost. The cost was prohibitive and there was no guarantee of meeting space. The other club was definitely interested until it was discovered that the church was interracial and more importantly that one of the ministers was a Negro. Then we tried to secure the sanctuary of the Seventh Day Adventist Church in the area. After a conference with the minister the whole idea collapsed.

Finally the local committee of the Presbytery became active in our behalf, acting as liaison between our Fellowship Church and the San Francisco Presbytery. They were able to effect an arrangement with the official representing the Methodist Episcopal Church of California. This arrangement made possible an exchange of meeting places between Fellowship Church and the Filipino Methodist Church. While we had been meeting from the beginning in property owned by the Presbyterian Church, in which the Japanese-American Presbyterian Church had functioned prior to the evacuation of the Japanese, the Filipino Methodist Church was meeting in property owned by the Methodist Episcopal Church in which the Japanese Methodist Church had worshipped before the evacuation. Since our group was larger than the Filipino Church, and their place of meeting was more commodious than ours, everybody was pleased with the exchange. The officials of the Presbyterian Church worked out the business arrangements with the official of the Methodist Episcopal Church and we were able to get the use of the sanctuary without any actual expenditure of money from our limited funds.

This building on Pine Street was located on the other side of the dividing line, Van Ness Avenue, which meant that to locate there would take the church out of the ghetto. It is irrelevant that we were less than two blocks from "the other side of the tracks." Moving outside of the ghetto gave to our beginning a freedom and a challenge which would never have been had we remained.

Now that we had a representative membership, a fellowship of people agreed on a simple commitment to a growing understanding of all men as sons of God, we were face to face with the radical choice either to become a Presbyterian church, to exist under the sponsorship of the Presbytery and so become a financially dependent mission of that church; or to become independent, losing temporarily at least any sense of belonging to any direct line or conventional lineage within the Christian family but with the way open for some future denominational affiliation.

The Presbyterian Church did not press us unduly. The board was patient and wise in permitting us time to make our decision. In a long conference with one of the officials I was convinced of the integrity of their concern and of the high motive which had inspired them to sponsor us originally. They were, nevertheless, the custodians of funds that had been given them for their church missions and so in all conscience they could not continue to support an enterprise that did not conform to the structure to which they were committed.

Still, and rightfully, some pressure was exerted upon us by the National Board of the Presbyterian Church, whose generosity had up to this time guaranteed our basic financial security. It is important, too, to point out that the logic of the situation should have moved us toward becoming a Presbyterian mission church. As such a mission we could have carried on an interracial program with a limited interracial membership but we would have suffered the many handicaps of being a mission. What was wrong with our becoming a mission? some timid souls had asked. As I saw it, should we continue as a mission of the Presbyterian Church, or of any denomination for that matter, we would to that extent be the object of charity and condescension. There would be those who would gladly and graciously cast their lot with us because they would want to help along a struggling interracial effort, without thereby challenging the segregated character of the denomination itself. The crippling disease that has dogged the vitality and the health of the Christian enterprise would have overtaken us—the deadly disease of condescension. Very quickly we would have become a dumping ground for uplifters and the challenge of the development of an integrated religious fellowship would have bounced off the conscience and hearts of the people. For herein lies the great temptation: *If a man can feel sorry for you, he can very easily absolve himself from dealing with you in any sense as an equal.* The spontaneous helpfulness arising out of a profound ethical concern can easily be twisted into a form of patronage under which human dignity cannot thrive.

We had to make a choice to become a Presbyterian church or to continue in the direction we had been going since our formal inaugural service. How could this be done on the basis of thoughtful consideration rather than much emotional reaction. It was discussion around this issue that very nearly destroyed the church even before it was formally organized.

The following letter was mailed to all members of record. It is self-explanatory. The date, July 1945.

To the members (commitment signers) of the Fellowship Church of All Peoples:

The Fellowship Church of All Peoples recognizes with gratitude the Christian concern of the Presbyterian Church with brotherhood as evinced in their being willing to back the organization and development of our Church up to the present time. We have arrived at the point at which it is necessary for us to decide about the future growth of our Church along lines that are more permanent and definitive as to organizational structure and denominational relations. From December 12, 1943, to the present time, our organization has been of a temporary nature. The Presbyterian Church up to the present time has provided a place for worship, a temporary apartment for one of the co-ministers, and an average contribution of $3600 a year towards the salaries of the co-ministers. We recognize with appreciation the significance of this expression of interest and good-will on their part.

The crucial questions before us as a Church are:

1. Is it our desire formally to become a Presbyterian church by consummating the kind of organization-affiliation that this requires?

2. Shall we become an independent (unaffiliated) church, interdenominational in character but autonomous and independent in denominational affiliation?

3. Shall we become an independent church, interdenominational in character and seek some kind of continuing relationship with the Presbyterian Church that pioneered our development?

We recognize the fact that it may have been in the minds of the

In This Commitment 49

Presbytery in consenting to sponsor our Church originally, that, in time, the Church would become Presbyterian in organization and affiliation. We recognize further that this intent has not been clear to those persons who have become a part of our fellowship during the months of our growth. We do not undertake the placing of responsibility for this. We point out the fact that there are at least five major denominations represented in our present membership, ignoring completely those persons among us who have had no previous denominational affiliation. We recognize further that more than $7000 have been contributed to our work since July 15, 1944, from persons who are members of major denominations other than Presbyterian, including Judaism.

If we become a Presbyterian church, it is reasonable to assume that we would have the continuous financial backing of that denomination until we are able to carry our own program financially. If we become independent and DID or DID NOT work out a relationship with Presbytery, it would be necessary for us to rethink our present program so as to adopt a budget that would be in keeping with our financial strength.

Please consider these proposals as carefully and as wisely as possible and register your opinion by checking the appended ballot. When the ballot is checked place it in the manila envelope and seal. Then place the sealed envelope in the white envelope and mail or leave it at the Church by Monday morning, July 30th. Be sure to put your name and address on the white envelope.

The ballots will be checked and the results determined in a congregational meeting called for Wednesday evening, August 1, 1359 Pine Street at 8 o'clock. Please circle this date on your calendar.

------------------ Tear or Cut here ----------------

BALLOT

1. I favor the plan of our consummating the organization of a Presbyterian church.
*2. I favor the plan of our consummating the organization of an independent church, inter-denominational in character without any relationship with any particular denomination.
*3. I favor the plan of our consummating the organization of an independent church, interdenominational in character with the request that we seek to discover a way through which other

religious groups and denominations may share in our venture—beginning with the historic denomination which pioneered us.

* (We assume that propositions 2 and 3 carry with them complete financial independence.)

The date was set for a congregational meeting at which all ballots that had been turned in were opened by a teller in the presence of the assembled congregation. They were read and tallied on a blackboard. When the total count was in, the vote was overwhelmingly in favor of independence. There was a very small margin of people in favor of our becoming a Presbyterian church. Most of the members voting did not wish us to cut ourselves off entirely from any organized group but checked the option which placed upon the organization the responsibility for working out ways and means for some kind of formal affiliation with an established denomination.

I shall never forget the night this fateful decision was made. Suddenly we were on our own without a roof over our heads, with no organized backing, but still with that dream in our hearts. There was a moment of panic—quiet, muted, glowing panic. As I sat there an experience I had had years before with my dog, Barriemore, rushed to my mind.

We were living on the campus at Howard University. Our house was surrounded by a yard enclosed by a picket fence about four feet high. There was a walk running along the side of the fence leading to the center of the campus. Barriemore would stretch out on the little porch before the front door and watch Western Union boys approaching our section of the sidewalk on their bicycles. When they came to the corner of our yard, Barriemore, safe inside the pickets, would meet them and bark them all the way along the fence until they moved beyond. This was very exciting exercise for him. One winter day after a heavy snowstorm, huge drifts had accumulated in the corners of the yard. A Western Union boy approached. Barriemore met him at the corner, but inside our yard, and as was his custom, barked him all the way to the next corner. This time, however, his momentum was so great that he ran up to the top of the snowdrift and, before he knew it, was over the fence on the sidewalk with nothing between him and the boy on the moving bicycle. Panic seized him—he stopped. But after that he could leap over the fence at will: the "take-off" from the snowdrift was not necessary.

We were like Barriemore, over the fence into the broad outside: we, too, knew panic!

Into the vacuum created by our decision a man, McKie Donnan, arose to speak. At the end of his statement that expressed his high hope, he offered a motion that a committee of nine be appointed (three Caucasians, three Negroes, two Japanese and one Chinese, as it turned out) to study our position and to make recommendations concerning purpose, goals, commitment, and the kind of organizational structure needed to implement such plans. The committee was enthusiastically appointed and meetings were begun immediately, twice weekly, for a minimum of two hours each time, under the guidance of a Canadian, Dr. Hugh MacMillan, a teacher-missionary on leave from his work in China, and stationed at the time in San Francisco working with a British commission. I had known him some twenty years previous when he and his wife were among a small group of young people who in 1925 spent ten days in a retreat in Pawling, New York, just prior to going to China to begin their work. During the retreat he was the leader of a Bible study group on the life of Jesus. He now saw into the beginnings of our undertaking quite prophetically and brought to the early stages of its development a gentle spirit, an incisive mind, a world outlook, and a profound religious conviction.

To be caught up in the kind of intensive searching which characterized this committee would have been reward enough, but to see timid people rise to their feet, affirming, rejecting, questioning; to watch bold people sit quietly with a newly earned respect for another's opinion—this was for me an exhilarating experience. Out of the vast fog of conversation slowly emerged the significant peaks. First,

THE DECLARATION

The Church for The Fellowship of All Peoples is a creative venture in interracial, intercultural, and interdenominational communion. In faith and genius it is Christian. While it derives its inspiration primarily from the source of Hebrew-Christian thought and life, it affirms the validity of spiritual insight wherever found and seeks to recognize, understand, and appreciate every aspect of truth whatever the channel through which it comes. It believes that human dignity is inherent in man as a creature of God, and it interprets the meaning of human life as essentially spiritual. It recognizes and affirms that the God of

Life and the God of Religion are one and the same, and that the normal relationship of people as children of one God and Father, is one of understanding, confidence, and fellowship.

And then,

THE MEMBERSHIP

The membership of the Church is open to any person who is willing to accept its commitment, to participate in its program, and to share in its responsibilities.

After that,

THE COMMITMENT

I affirm my need for a growing understanding of all men as sons of God, and seek after a vital interpretation of God as revealed in Jesus of Nazareth whose fellowship with God was the foundation of his fellowship with men.

I desire to have a part in the unfolding of the ideal of Christian fellowship through the union of men and women of varying national, cultural, racial, or creedal heritage in church communion.

I desire the strength of corporate worship with the imperative of personal dedication to the working out of God's purposes here and in all places which will be found through membership in this Church for the Fellowship of All Peoples.[2]

And finally,

THE COMMISSION

This Church undertakes to make specific impact upon the community through a membership committed to the application of the principles of the Church for the Fellowship of All Peoples in everyday living.

Each member is called upon to find his avenue of practical expression in fulfilling the Commitment both in his individual life and through active participation in the program of the Church.

After six weeks and a total of twelve committee meetings and six congregational meetings, here we were—a church with an inspired purpose and a creative commitment.

Now that we were a responsible functioning entity, it was necessary to assess our total position. The problems of finances, meaningful membership, programming, adequate space and facilities—these all loomed large and forbidding. Financially, we

[2] See page 158 for the Commitment now in use.

were in a state of shock! In the first place, we were no longer entitled to the contribution from the Presbytery of $300 a month for salaries as well as a meeting place and living quarters for me as the full-time minister. However, there were many individuals and groups who were interested enough in what we were trying to do to support the venture, in little ways and in big ways. Prior to my coming to San Francisco many people whom I had told of my concern were interested in having a continuing share in this undertaking, and I had brought with me more than $1200 which had been given me for the cause. A few months after I arrived in San Francisco, a Jewish lady from New York City, who had become interested in the idea as I had presented it to her before coming West, made a substantial contribution to the work we proposed to do with children. The interesting phrase she used was that she was glad to contribute to this "Christian experiment in democracy."

During our first year in San Francisco, the oldest Jewish synagogue west of the Mississippi River, a large Reformed congregation in San Francisco, invited me, through its spiritual leader Rabbi Irving Reichert, to preach at a Friday evening service. A few days after that service the Rabbi came to pay me a visit. He expressed profound interest in this fellowship ideal, and had real insight into its meaning. As he was leaving he handed me an envelope and a letter expressing in beautiful language the attitude of his congregation. When I looked into the envelope there were several checks; the total amounted to $1500. This was their contribution, without strings and without involvement beyond a spiritual concern for the welfare of a dream. In addition to this, the Rabbi offered me the use of an office in the Temple so that I would have a place to read and write and spend time for quiet reflection. During all the years, there has been the closest relationship between these two congregations with mutual exchange of pulpits and many other expressions of a deep spiritual fellowship.

Various other persons and groups in the city of San Francisco contributed to maintaining our independence. One person made a substantial personal gift to be used as part of the purchase price of a permanent home for the Thurman family—a house that would also be used as a meeting place for all group activities of the church except the Sunday worship services.

During this initial period and throughout the remaining years, I was under a great necessity to use all of my physical resources not only to raise money for the church but also to secure enough funds to supplement my own salary to make ends meet. Each winter I returned East, speaking and preaching several times a day and spending each night on the train so as to make the next day's engagements. For weeks on end it was a series of one- and two-day stands. This is stated simply for the record.

After we were formally organized and had adopted the official name, "The Church for the Fellowship of All Peoples," we were incorporated as a church under the laws of the State of California. Further, we sought membership in, and were received by, the San Francisco Council of Churches. But one of the first problems, which is still present at this writing, had to do with our "status" as a church.

I had known theoretically that Christianity as a religion is *adjectival* in character; that is, there is no such thing as a church, as such, without denominational description—it has to be some kind of church—Methodist, Baptist, Congregational, or what not. In other words, the organizational genius of Christianity is sectarian. If we were to continue as an independent religious fellowship, our greatest temptation would be to multiply ourselves on the basis of program and commitment and thereby become another denomination. Again and again, people would raise the question, "When you join Fellowship Church, what do you join?" The only answer we could give was that they were joining The Church for the Fellowship of All Peoples. We were a religious fellowship dedicated to the worship of God and the kind of common life that that worship inspired. This meant the precarious process of developing experimentally, within a general tradition, a polity, a program, and a basis for continuity.

We felt under the necessity of evolving certain ceremonials that best fitted our common religious experience. We decided we would have a special communion service each year on the Sunday designated as World-Wide Communion Sunday. This was one point at which we could be a part of the Church Universal at its highest point of ceremonial celebration. At other times during the year, when the need was deeply felt, special communion services would be held. There was to be no baptismal ceremony. On this there was complete agreement because within our membership there were at least eight major denominations represented. I am sure that if we had been confronted with a demand for baptism, it would have been handled by the group sympathetically and intelligently.

One of the practical matters provided for in our by-laws was dual membership. Simply stated, this provision made it possible for a person to become a member of Fellowship Church and at the same time hold his membership in the church of his upbringing. Among the group in the original fellowship were persons who were also active in local churches in San Francisco, but who were convinced that their particular church was either unable or unwilling to deal with the concept of inclusive membership and were thereby attracted to such an experience in Fellowship Church. This was one way of providing systematically experiences of unity that transcended creedal as well as national lines.

The dual membership arrangement was looked upon with suspicion by some churches in the community—and quite naturally. There was the notion that inasmuch as we were a new group, we had seized upon a subtle device for taking members from other churches. We were, nevertheless, assured of the rightness of our plan—a plan which operated, for the most part, very simply.

In the beginning, the categories were "members" and "associate members," a classification indicated by the individual member himself. As far as our records were concerned, there was no difference in the status of the two kinds of members. A little later, the category "associate member" became "resident," and members in distant places became "national associates." Finally the membership was divided simply into resident members, and members-at-large. A resident member is a member of the church who lives in the San Francisco Bay Area. He may be carrying a dual membership. Members-at-large are all members of the church who do not live in the Bay Area. When a resident member moves out of the Bay Area, he becomes automatically a member-at-large.

As it developed, the purpose of the dual membership was twofold. First it provided an opportunity for people who lived in San Francisco and were active in local "segregated" churches to experience a racially-integrated fellowship, religious in character. They would thus be able to share this experience in the church of their original fellowship. This aspect of the intent has not altogether fulfilled its promise. Some members found it increasingly difficult to divide their loyalties and were unwilling to make a teaching instrument out of their personal religious aspirations and experiences. For them in one or the other of the churches, theirs would become merely a token membership. There were, however, conspicuous exceptions.

For instance, there was one person who was a member of the Society of Friends. She and her family became more and more involved in the life of Fellowship Church. In time she became a most active and influential member of the board. Periodically, however, she would absent herself from Fellowship Church, giving her attendance and time to the demands of her birthright religious faith.

I recall another person in a different category. She was most active in the church until it was fully organized. After that she came to see me to explain that she could no longer be a part of our fellowship because her denomination strictly forbade her to be a member of any other church.

Among the many spirits of the earlier period there was one lady who was the vice-chairman of the women's organization of Grace Cathedral, but who, until her death, was an acknowledged leader in our fellowship. It was she who arranged a dinner meeting with me and the sainted Bishop Parsons in order to have me discuss my ideas with him. It was important for her that he understand and support what we were doing. From that initial meeting he became our friend; he was always a welcome and inspiring guest in our pulpit.

The second purpose of dual membership was to provide some way by which people who lived in different parts of America and the world might be related to the development of this dream in San Francisco, as participating individuals. Through them the idea behind our venture would spread, and men and women who were despairing of the church in this aspect would be lifted up and strengthened. This second purpose fulfilled its promise: a few years after the church was under way there were about one thousand such members in the United States, Canada, England, Formosa, South Africa, and Japan. Many of these members-at-large made it a point to include a visit to the church as a regular part of their trips to San Francisco or to the West Coast.

There are on record several instances of whole groups sharing a kind of "collective-membership-at-large." For many years prior

In This Commitment

to my moving to California, I had been a regular lecturer or preacher on various college and school campuses. These contacts were continued and in some instances intensified after I began my work in San Francisco. As I used each opportunity to carry the word concerning the church and its development, there followed naturally an interest which expressed itself in various ways. Phillips Academy at Andover, Massachusetts, used our commitment as an important guide in establishing the basis of membership in the school church. Many of the students and some of the faculty were members-at-large of Fellowship Church. For several years, the Masters School of Dobbs Ferry, New York, and the Emma Willard School of Troy, New York, to mention only two, through their student organizations, were active supporters of the work of the church. Very often during the summers students with their parents included a weekend in San Francisco as a part of their trip West. All of this is to say that wherever I went to speak or to preach, the message of the church was carried. In homes in Boston, Philadelphia, Germantown, Chicago, Washington, D.C., members-at-large invited special groups in to hear reports on the development of the church and to share in its contagion.

One of the unexplored areas of the ministry of the church is the development of a program which will include this national and international constituency without at the same time moving in the direction of a denomination. This plan belongs to the second decade of the development of the church. It is simple to use members-at-large for purposes of fund-raising and publicity, but to involve them in some kind of growing experience takes the kind of imagination, boldness, and daring thought that is now beginning to evolve.

In the early years a person became a member of the church by indicating his wish to sign the commitment. There was no ceremony to mark the event. Although becoming a member certainly had a private, conscious significance, there was also a need for celebrating the act of coming into the church. Thus, our first high moment of dedication come on the Sunday following the inaugural service when the "charter" members signed the commitment in a special ceremony of recognition. After this, applicants who applied for commitments mailed them back to the ministers who in turn gave them to the secretary of the board. Then the following Sunday the new members came forward and were inducted by a series of responses between themselves and the congregation. While this was not quite adequate and seemed in some ways artificial and unreal, still it led to an established custom. One of the members gave the church a large, handsome leather-bound membership book which made it possible for each member to register his name as having already signed and deposited the commitment with the church officials. It was easy then to make the signing of the book an impressive public ceremony.

The plan as it is now established is that any person interested in membership meets with the membership committee to discuss the history and concept of the church. Its organizational structure is explained, the financial responsibility of the member is examined, and at the same time arrangements are made for his financial pledge to the church. This is a very permissive session with all questions freely discussed. Then the new member has a personal conference with the minister at which time the meaning of the commitment and its significance in the life of the individual is interpreted thoroughly. The final stage is the signing of the book of membership in the presence of the congregation at a regular Sunday morning service. The member being inducted comes forward and is greeted by the chairman of the membership committee who is standing by the podium on which the book rests. When the new member signs his name in the book, a piece of ivy is pinned to his lapel as a symbol of "the growing edge" which has come to be the effective motto of the church. The minister then leads the entire congregation in a moment of rededication with everyone standing together reading the commitment aloud. At the close of the service there is a special coffee hour during which the minister again introduces the new members so that old members may have a chance to welcome each one personally. The new communicants are easily distinguished because of the ivy symbol. Through the years some of the members have planted the ivy in their homes as a growing symbol of their own life, and of their commitment to the church.

One of the healthiest aspects of the growth in membership was the fact that more than 90 per cent of the members inducted in the course of a year were persons who had been attending the church regularly for a period of from three months to a year or more. This indicated that the act of joining was the result of a mature decision on their part rather than an emotional response to a whim. Occasionally a person visited the church once and was so impressed with what he saw and felt that he wanted to join immediately. Whether the policy was wise or not may be debatable but I definitely discouraged that kind of decision. Invariably I advised the individual to wait long enough to attend the church, to observe and share in its work, to become acquainted with the members and to realize religious experience with them. Only then, I urged, should he succeed to the formal status of membership. I recall only one person who, after waiting, decided against coming into the church immediately; but within a year after my leaving San Francisco, he did join.

A study of the membership roll of Fellowship Church reveals that we are constantly dealing with a marginal turnover. It is customary to prune the membership list about every six months. If a person has not been in attendance for some time and has shown no signs of participating in our experience, he is interviewed, if possible, before being placed on the inactive list. This marginal turnover in the early days was attributed to several factors. Service men and women were stationed in and around San Francisco for varying and limited periods of time; they were members on the move. Some people were constantly on the move because of the demands of their jobs during the war years and immediately afterward. Others experienced profound disappointment in the church because it was a *church* and not merely a social-protest group. Some people felt that they had to have more conventional forms of church life; they missed the traditional symbolism and rituals with which they had been familiar at an earlier period in their lives. Others who attempted to carry dual membership found that the inconvenience of distance could be resolved only with a decision to remain with the church of their earlier years.

I viewed this marginal turnover in very positive terms. To me it meant that every person who had become a part of the church and had later separated himself from it had been exposed to the experience of our particular kind of fellowship, and to that extent would have his own faith confirmed in the practicability of a church relationship in which there would be no cultural and racial barriers. This seems to me perhaps the most crucial and valuable contribution of the church itself. It is a common experience for me to meet people all over the United States who say, "I was a member of Fellowship Church for the ten months I was in California, and it has made all the difference to me in how I feel about people."

In the very beginning the membership was made up almost exclusively of adults. There were few families, as such. As families began coming to the church there was a demand for a ceremonial "dedication of children." The ceremony we developed focused attention on the responsibility of parents to train their children in accordance with the religious faith most meaningful to them and in the light of which the family lived its life. During the entire period of my ministry at the church this ceremony was used. At the conclusion of the ceremony a copy of it, signed by the minister, was given to the family as their permanent record, and the name of the baby and the date of the dedication were inscribed in the church register. Often parents who themselves were not members of the church asked to have their babies dedicated. I always agreed. In many instances, the parents followed their child's dedication by becoming members.

It was important not only to keep ever before us the meaning of our commitment but also to keep ourselves reminded that while the mood in which we functioned was experimental, what we were undertaking, at its very depth, was not an experiment.

There is a perpetual dilemma which constantly faces any creative movement of the spirit: If the movement is to last, it must somehow be caught and embodied in concrete manifestation. And yet when it is embodied in a concrete form like an organization or an institution, the vitality tends to disintegrate. The power that saves it, finally destroys it. If the movement survives, it must constantly spill over, break out in a new, fresh way, or it dies. It is interesting that in this connection certain of the founding fathers of our country insisted that if we were to survive with a vital government, the right to redefine, to restate the original insight, must be forever protected. We were urged aright to resist all tyrannies that may arise because they would mean the end of the growth and development of the dream which is ours. If the dream or the movement is deeply involved in a more specific revelation of God to the children of men, then all of this is even more binding than political organization assumes. We faced the constant danger of becoming so fenced in by the organization that the very spirit we sought to transmit was in constant jeopardy. It was necessary to test every aspect of our organization by the spirit of our central undertaking. This testing meant holding all aspects of our structure before God in worship and commitment to protect ourselves from being wedded to a plan or a scheme for its own sake alone. Testing and experimenting, experimenting and testing, this was our working paper. Again, there must be no distinction between the demand made upon our organization and the demands made upon our lives and character. I was convinced that there was no substitute for the direct obligation to test our motives, our interests, our daily living, by the spirit of God which first sent us on our way in this glorious adventure. And to do this without self-righteousness or any show of piety. Membership in the church must not sanction a kind of behavior in our human relations that denies our commitment to God as He gives us light to understand it.

From the beginning the atmosphere of the church was very permissive, quite in keeping with the experience of equality which was always our goal. This kind of equality was not derived from status, ability, or gifts of any kind whatsoever, but was rooted in the sense of infinite worth by which each person truly regarded himself. To translate this into *social* worth defined the task of the church in the world.

Once, before I was leaving for a six-week trip East for lecturing, preaching, and fund-raising, a very dramatic thing happened. As Dr. Fisk moved to the pulpit to give the benediction, and all heads were bowed, in the split second before his quiet words were uttered the silence was broken by a very familiar voice saying, "Forgive me, Dr. Fisk, ladies and gentlemen: our pastor is going away this afternoon for more than a month. While he is away he will be working for us. Back where I grew up, when the pastor went away even on vacation we always gave him a special offering. Now when Dr. Thurman goes into the dining car to get his dinner they don't care that he is a great preacher and that he is our pastor and that we love him very much. They'll just want to know if he has enough money to pay for the dinner he orders. So, I am putting a dollar bill on the table and all of you who feel as I do, I want you to come up and add your money to it."

Dr. Fisk rose to the occasion by saying, "After the benediction, any persons who may want to respond to what Mrs.———has said may do so."

It was never my custom to greet people at the door at the close of the service but on this particular Sunday I did. When I had shaken hands with the congregation and everyone had gone except me, the lady found me and put an envelope in my hand containing the gift for my trip. She said, "I hope I didn't embarrass you by what I did, but the spirit moved in me and I had to act."

I thanked her by saying, "If the time ever comes in this church when you are no longer free to respond in deeds to the movement of the Spirit of God in your heart, then our church is no longer the church of God."

When I returned after several weeks, at a regular board meeting one of the members spoke with great feeling about the incident. He was distressed because he felt that people who spoke out of turn and with such liberty should be curbed. He offered a motion to the effect that the chairman of the board should advise the lady in question that this was not the kind of church in which such things happened.

Before there was a second to the motion I asked and received permission to speak:

"I understand the intent of the motion but I want to say something before it is voted on. Of course, I was a bit embarrassed to have a collection taken to give to me for my trip. But I was profoundly stirred by the spirit of the whole incident. Over and over again, I said, 'Thank God for a fellowship like ours in which a person feels free enough to do such a thing.' Mrs.———was seated with Dr.———, a Ph.D. in psychology from Stanford University. As a matter of fact, they were sharing the same hymn book. Here were two extremes in our fellowship, both worshiping and sharing in their own way. As I said on that Sunday to the lady in question, 'If the time ever comes in this church when you are no longer free to respond in deeds to the movement of the Spirit of God in your heart, then our church is no longer the church of God.'"

Ministers officiating at the "inaugural" ceremony of Fellowship Church, Sunday, October 8, 1944: (standing, left to right) Dr. Buell G. Gallagher, Co-pastor, South Berkeley Community Church; Rabbi Elliot M. Burstein, Chairman, Northern California Board of Rabbis and Cantors; Dr. John C. Leffler, President, San Francisco Council of Churches; (seated) Co-pastors Dr. Howard Thurman and Dr. Alfred G. Fisk. (page 41)

Under the leadership of the Church Board (below) and its chairman, Gene Walker (seated at head of table), the present church building (right) was purchased in January 1949. The sanctuary is on the second floor, offices and Fellowship Hall on the ground floor.

Religious education for adults has centered in small study groups, such as the one being conducted here by Dr. Thurman.

At a Christmas-Chanukah party—sponsored jointly by the Intercultural Workshop and the Committee on Religious Education—children light Chanukah candles beside the Christmas tree.

Photo by E. F. Joseph

A group from the Intercultural Workshop of Fellowship Church, including representatives of five ethnic or national backgrounds, traveled at their own expense to a Plenary Session of UNESCO in Paris. Shown in the picture are the internationally known Quintette, under the direction of Corinne Barrow Williams (seated, extreme left). Included also are Lynn Buchanan (standing, extreme left), Executive Director of Fellowship Church, and Sue Bailey Thurman (seated, center), Chairman of the Intercultural Workshop.

A student-madonna in the "Worship through Art and Music" series presented by Dr. Thurman when he was Dean of the Chapel at Howard University. A similar program at Fellowship Church featured madonnas from twelve nationalities.

Scurlock Photo

The Liturgical Dance Choir interpreting the experience of meditation: the solitary figure symbolizes the individual while the dancers represent various aspects of the process of "centering down" in meditation.

Weddings large or small are intimate, and the beauty and sanctity of the occasion are always preserved. The two church members being married (right) carry large community responsibilities.

With Mrs. Thurman at a dinner in honor of the Thurmans in August, 1954 are Mrs. Dryden Phelps (left), wife of the interim minister (1953–1955), and Rev. and Mrs. Cyril Grant of Rotherham, England, whose wedding was performed at Fellowship Church. Mrs. Grant, a native Californian, was one of the first secretaries of the church.

Cox Studio

Cox Studio

Rev. Francis Geddes, the present minister, greets Mrs. Phyllis Williams, the senior member of Fellowship Church, on Easter Sunday morning, 1959.

3. The Letter and the Spirit

AFTER THE EVACUATION PERIOD ended and the Japanese-Americans returned to San Francisco and to their churches, it was necessary for us to leave the Japanese Methodist Church building and find another meeting place. For our Sunday services we were able to rent the auditorium of the Little Theatre on Washington Street, which had been erected as a church in the first place. We had the use of it between the hours of ten and two, for the morning worship and the coffee hour following. The office of the church was a small room in another building several blocks away. All of the group meetings of the church were now established in the Thurman home on California Street. Board meetings, study groups, choir rehearsals, drama and intercultural workshops—these were held there. Fortunately there was room enough in the spacious house to take care of these varied activities without completely destroying our family privacy.

It was here the programs were planned to promote the letter and spirit of our commitment. For the first six months or so of 1945 the two activities of the church were Sunday morning worship and our summer camp for children. So significant and successful was the children's camp that gifts from a friend in New York City and from the local Rosenberg Foundation underwrote the salary of a full-time leader to develop the intercultural aspects of our whole children's program, which became our Junior Intercultural Workshop. Its guiding philosophy was to expose the children of this diverse group to one another's national, cultural, and ethnic background and to help each to appreciate his own cultural heritage, the gift from his parents.

The sponsorship of the children's program was included in the work of the church's Intercultural Committee. Afternoons after school and for a half-day on Saturday, for two years, the children came to the Workshop studio in the basement of the Thurman home. The committee modeled its plan on the international summer camp that had preceded it. Games, pictures, slides, stories, excursions—all these helped the children to understand the particular group being studied—and remember, always several children were members of that particular group. Unfortunately, however, there was no space in the Little Theatre for Sunday work with the children, so it was not possible at this time to include this program in the children's religious instruction. The problems involved in such religious instruction away from the building where regular religious worship took place seemed insurmountable. Then, too, many of the parents of the children in the workshop were not actively associated with Fellowship Church. Our concern was to give a broad cultural experience to children of the San Francisco community in a natural setting as a normal part of their growth and interests. We wanted this test to discover if it could be done by using materials that would be available to any group which had the interest, the concern, and the point of view necessary.

Because this program was underwritten, it was very difficult for the church members to realize that the Workshop was an integral part of their own commitment. Their difficulty was not remarkable because it merely emphasized the narrowness of the worlds in which the adults themselves lived. We then felt we had to undertake the very serious job of educating our adult members to understand and appreciate the total commitment. It was soon all too apparent that just with the adults alone the members of the Intercultural Committee, being adults themselves, would have their work cut out for them.

The purpose of the committee's work with adults was to add a hard core of facts and information to the good will already manifest in the church members. The most effective plan the committee used in the early years was a series of periodic international Fellowship Church dinners. The motif of each dinner, being intergroup or intercultural in character, attracted a cross section of the city of San Francisco. Our congregation will always remember the Filipino dinner when the whole room was decorated with imitation plants and flowers indigenous to the Islands, all of which were made by "church artists" from varicolored paper. The menu had among its several entrees a chicken dish, Filipino style. The program included native music by excellent musicians from the Filipino community, including a children's choir; and a woman educator who had come directly from Manila gave the group new insights into the hopes of Filipinos in the Islands and on the mainland of the United States.

When the ban against the Japanese-Americans was lifted and they had begun to return in groups to the West Coast, a dinner was given in their honor with principal speakers representing the brave men of the 442nd Battalion who had so distinguished themselves in the campaigns in Europe. Then there was the East Indian meal, and the program offered by an old friend, an executive secretary of the Student Christian Movement of India, Dr. Ralla Ram, whom we had known in his own country. He was on a lecture tour. During the organization of the United Nations a dinner was held in honor of the men and women of the National Negro Press who were covering the sessions. There was the deepest appreciation for the gift of these special guests who shared with us the experience and philosophy of writers who were among the chief molders of public opinion in the Negro communities across the nation. Always the same basic purpose, notice, was to expose the church members and their friends to the life, the culture, the hopes of people who have come from everywhere to form the corporate strength of American society.

Among other activities the committee conducted a series of forum discussions, lectures, recitals, and art exhibits designed to carry out the same broad purposes. Chang Shu-Chi, a Chinese artist who had painted a picture, the two hundred doves of peace for the city of Washington, D.C., demonstrated the technique of modern Oriental painting. A well-known concert artist from the East, Camille Nickerson, gave an interpretation of early life in New Orleans in a program of Creole songs. Books of factual and technical material were added to the church library for those who wanted to read further. The claim is not made here that the program as outlined above was or is unique except in one particular. It was an integral part of the context of the religious experience and the social fellowship of the church itself. Slowly there began to emerge a climate in which the fruits of culture could be appreciated, assimilated, and shared without patronage or condescension.

Christian churches in their far-flung missionary enterprises have been engaged in cultural education for many generations, but too often without any marked increase in the respect its church members show for individuals who come from the lands and cultures to which the missionary enterprise has been carried. For all of the efforts, something has constantly misfired. Missionaries taught others to understand our culture, but failed to teach us the cultures they had met. This very lack created an attitude of regarding people of other cultures merely as possible proselytes. They stood out as people for whom something was being done primarily on behalf of the denominational faith alone, and they were understood primarily in relation to the particular faith, but never in relation to *their own fact*. What a difference that combination of the two would have made to the future peace of the world! Here again we make no claim as to the success of this program; but we would establish the fact that we were attempting to place an understanding mind at the very center of the good will inspired by our worship of God. It was a means of informing our good will with knowledge *of*, as a corrective to knowledge *about*.

Perhaps the most dramatic activity of the Intercultural Committee was the delegation sent from Fellowship Church to attend an annual plenary session of UNESCO in Paris. Mrs. Thurman as chairman of the Intercultural Committee and Lynn Buchanan as executive director of Fellowship Church were co-chairmen of this unique delegation composed of three Negroes, one Mexican-American, one Japanese-American, one Chinese-American, and six Caucasians. The group included the Fellowship Church Quintet which was to represent the church in a series of concerts in Europe. Each member of the group financed himself. Of course, the group had no official standing on the trip because there was no way by which a church could have official representation at a meeting of UNESCO. However, the experience was a very illuminating one for the party itself as well as for the church congregation, for the community of San Francisco, and for national and international members-at-large.

The delegation traveled across the country from San Francisco to New York in a station wagon caravan. As they sought places to eat and sleep they experienced in several instances the tragic consequences of racial prejudice and discrimination. On board the *Queen Mary* the Quintet gave a full evening concert as guests of the ship's officers. The first stop was London where a concert was presented in the YWCA auditorium. In London, too, a chance came to visit several international members-at-large of the Fellowship congregation. The entire delegation was there except the Japanese-American member who for technical reasons was not permitted to land in England but had to go on alone to Paris. In Paris they attended all of the sessions of the UNESCO conference and in addition, the Quintet appeared in the Artists' Series sponsored by the American Church of Paris, and later presented a concert at the University of Paris.

When they returned and were en route back to San Francisco, public meetings were held for them in New York City, Philadelphia, and Cleveland at which the group gave an interpretation of the meaning of their experience. In San Francisco, through individual and group reports, much was done to focus the minds of many people on the meaning and significance of the UNESCO program. The effect of the trip on the congregation in many significant ways continues to be marked.

The fellowship Church Quintet was one flowering of the evolution of our music program, now a major vehicle for the congregation's self-expression and worship.

It was not until we moved into our own building on Larkin Street that we were able to have the use of an organ. Our first choral unit was made up of people who for the most part were semi-professionals and who sang on occasion when there was a special service. Of course, no sound foundation in music could be established in this way. What we needed was one person, competent and skilled, who would be in a position to devote enough time to develop a singing unit from among the members of the congregation itself. Our first choral director, Mrs. Joseph James, was indeed competent and skilled, but unable to remain with us long enough to do a sustained and effective job.

The year before Mrs. James left I was invited to be one of the Good Friday speakers at the First Congregational Church downtown. The wife of the tenor soloist, himself a concert artist, was very much impressed with a certain quotation which I had read in my sermon. The correspondence which developed as a result of this incident caused me to turn to her for advice in finding an able person to develop a choir for Fellowship Church. She told me about Mrs. Corrinne Williams who lived and taught voice in Stockton but who had a studio in San Francisco as well. I went to see her. I explained my mission, detailing as fully as possible the concept and the dream which were ours, with the hope that she might be willing to offer her tremendous gifts to us. I was in a position to offer a very modest monthly stipend made possible by the interest of a personal friend of mine, Todd Duncan, the nationally known concert artist, who guaranteed the sum of fifty dollars a month for six months to help pay the salary of the person whom we might secure. I shall always remember the interview. In the middle of my story she thanked me for coming, but asked if I would leave and return in a week's time. She said, "If I hear you out, I'll say 'Yes' now and perhaps regret it as soon as you've walked out of the door."

Within the week I was back ringing her doorbell. My hopes were soaring but I dared not give in to them. There was some delay in answering. I decided that she was not at home and was regarding this as a kind of reprieve. At that moment the door was opened with pointed enthusiasm. I looked in her face and there written large and clear was my answer. My heart stirred within me. She showed me to a chair, took one herself—but I remained standing. I wanted to hear the words. They came. "I have decided to come with you. After thinking about it I know that at such a critical time in the world no one, least of all the artist, can afford the luxury of the side lines. I do not know, but I think this is the kind of opportunity I have been seeking for a long time.

"I must have time to clear up a few things and to give notice to the church in Stockton. I think I can do it in a month. I have some excellent voice students and I will bring a few of them with me as the nucleus of the choir I'll develop."

Over coffee we let our fancy range far and wide over many things. As goes the saying, "I left walking on air."

During the first six months of her work as choral director, we were unable to buy any of the needed music, so she bought the music out of her own pocket. The choir soon became the very examplar of the intergroup character of our communion. There were persons representing several ethnic and cultural groups, several denominations, and more than one faith. The choir members became increasingly involved in the commitment of the church, and most of them became members. The quality of the music was superior to that found in many formal institutions of worship. Its vitality and enthusiasm spread through the congregation, so that soon our congregational singing became outstanding. The Quintet, though professional, was a natural development of the church itself with each member making vital contributions in other departments of the church as well. The personnel of the Quintet was an ambulatory example of the basic concept upon which our church was built: experiences of spiritual unity were more compelling than the things that divide. It was made up of Americans—Mexican, Chinese, Negro—one man of Dutch background, and Mrs. Williams herself.

The ministry of music was not confined to the development of worship in our own congregation alone. The service of the group to the program of the Conference of Christians and Jews in the city was so significant one year that our church received a special Brotherhood Award. Wherever civic, cultural, or church groups gathered in public meetings to focus their thoughts on living together in a brotherhood crossing all barriers of race, class, or creed, the choir and the Quintet of Fellowship Church, each through its music and its intergroup character, contributed creatively to the occasions.

After some years, when Corrinne Williams, the inspired director who had planned and trained this fine choir, became ill and could no longer carry on her work with us, a natural choice as her successor was her foremost pupil and protégé, a young Chinese baritone, Raymond Fong. It would be my guess that Fellowship Church is the only non-Chinese-American church in the United States whose distinguished choir director is a Chinese-American. Not only has the choir presented through the years fresh, worshipful, and beautiful anthems for the Sunday service, but at least once annually it performs a major work. Three times within a period of four years it presented the celebrated oratorio, *The Ordering of Moses*, by the Negro composer, the late R. Nathaniel Dett, and other choral works of equal merit and distinction.

Now that we had excellent music, and a stable congregation in a fixed place of worship, we could see the emergence of a definite theory of worship. The basic conception was that the highest act of celebration of the human spirit is the worship of God. In the act of worship the worshiper sees himself as being in the presence of God. In His presence the worshiper is neither male nor female, black nor white, Protestant nor Catholic nor

Buddhist nor Hindu, but a human spirit laid bare, stripped to whatever there is that is literal and irreducible. This kind of worship inspires a quality of life that makes barriers of separateness among men increasingly and finally untenable. Worship therefore is central in the church.

In my judgment the most significant result in the Fellowship Church communion is not the participation in the fellowship by a cross section of people, but rather it is the quality of the individual's religious experience achieved through worship and the effect of that experience on daily behavior. Worship is at once the source and the dynamics both of religious inspiration and judgment. From the very beginning the high point in each week was the Sunday morning worship service. It is so designed that there is for each person present *a* moment which becomes *his* moment in the presence of God. It may be in the hymns or in the silence, in the music, the reading of the Scripture, the speaking of the word, the period of prayer and meditation. Among the congregation there must be a moment which becomes intensely personal and private for each worshiper. The order of service, carefully devised, is largely nonritualistic. In my opinion the most important part of the service is the period of meditation preceding the sermon. Here the congregation and the minister become still in the presence of God. This is the time when the innermost secrets of life are laid bare without pretense, when each one of us feels that he is in the presence of One who understands thoroughly and completely and in whose presence it is unnecessary to pretend anything. Out of the period of meditation there comes a high resolve, and a sense of being cleansed; sometimes there is the conviction of sin; but most often there arises hope and confidence for what awaits in the next turning of the road. At first the congregation experienced some difficulty in being thrown so fully upon its own life and need without the customary voicing of the formal pastoral prayer. But more and more this quiet time has become a moment of rare and holy celebration.

It was about three years after our beginning that we also began experimenting with a meditation period that came before, and was distinctly separate from, the regular service. I included in a monthly letter to the congregation the plan of the experiment. Then the idea was discussed with the congregation informally at a Sunday coffee hour. All persons interested in such an experiment were asked to come to church a half hour before the service. The procedure was simple. At first, I conducted the period standing in the pulpit throughout the silence as well as during the spoken words of guidance. Eventually there was less need for direction; I remained seated in the pulpit to dramatize further the fact that we were all a company of persons together seeking to know for ourselves the will of God.

Soon I discovered that I would have to continue searching for the best way to offer that half hour to the many individuals not accustomed to meditation. I began writing, almost always in the first person, a provocative and suggestive affirmation for meditation. This was mimeographed and given to each person as he came into the service. Thus there was available, directly for each one, something in the nature of a pump primer. If the individual could not somehow find a beginning of his own, here was an evocative idea which might summon his thoughts and engage his spirit. These affirmations were widely used. During the war, members of the congregation sent hundreds of copies to men and women in the armed services. The procedure finally worked out this way: promptly at ten-thirty the organist would play for ten or twelve minutes. At first the music had a mood quality with no recognizable melodies. Once the group had felt the mood music, it was then helpful to play familiar but undistracting hymn tunes. The music served a dual purpose: it inspired meditation and it gave cover to those coming late. After the music ceased, it was understood that no one was to come into the sanctuary until the remaining period of complete silence was over. During the very last moments of the half hour, I summarized in two or three sentences thoughts that had come out of my own meditation, the organist picked up the theme again, I withdrew and the meditation service was over. Generally there was a five-minute interval between that service and the beginning of the regular morning service of worship. This quiet period became one of the most dynamic sources of vitality in the life of the church. Again and again the quality of this first period of meditation would carry over into the briefer second meditation during the morning service. The earlier period was also useful because often there came to individuals illuminations of their own problems which made it unnecessary for them to seek any other help. At no time was it ever necessary to urge people to attend this earlier service. Although written meditations are no longer used, many continue to share the benefits of this service.

The Sunday morning sermon also played an important part in the development of the religious life and ministry of the congregation. During my ministry I did nothing to fit my sermons to the calendar of the Christian year, as important as this can be and is in some congregations. The only high moments of the year I emphasized were Passion Week and Christmas. In the sermons, the major emphasis was on interpreting the meaning of religious experience and providing thoughtful content for reflection. The sermon was used to instruct, to inform, to challenge, to inspire, but always to dedicate and commit life to God. I discovered that the most useful method was to present in sequence an extended series of sermons dealing with various aspects of the same basic insight.

If religious experience in a person's life is to be effective, it must start with a hard core of purpose and with a definite plan. In many churches, the tendency is to take the latter for granted. As our participation in worship became more and more meaningful, we found ourselves wanting to provide ideas to challenge and inform the mind. To accomplish this end we had to draw upon the past to enhance the quality of our strivings in the present. We also found it useful to appropriate from all the disciplines of knowledge that which contributed to our purposes. Furthermore, when it came to action, if we were well-informed before we knocked, many different doors would open to us.

We met this need for stimulating the mind in two ways, by the sermon and the study group. We were a very heterogeneous group. Not only had we come from a variety of cultural backgrounds, but we were heterogeneous because of the religious orientation in our background. Many of our members had come into the church from various denominations in which they had been active workers. There were Episcopalians, Presbyterians, Baptists, and several kinds of Methodists, Saints of Christ, and others. A way had to be found to help all of these people. The content of the sermons has to be informative and instructive. At the same time they had to convey a sense of the Eternal. It was necessary that the total setting of worship and its total content would enable the worshipers to sense the historical roots of religious experience and to understand the flowering of beliefs, creeds, and commitments.

I found one of the most effective ways was to preach a series of sermons dealing with many aspects of human experience and spiritual insight. To the limit of my own competency, I drew on all of the resources of a lifetime of study, meditation, and experience.

Let me give you four examples:

a. A series of sermons on "The Sermon on the Mount" provided an opportunity not only to bring into sharp focus the overwhelming ethical imperative of the Christian religion, but also to teach a great deal about the Old Testament in order better to understand the words of Jesus. Sometimes a series would extend over eight or nine weeks. Occasionally in the course of the series, I would call attention to a particular book which I urged the congregation to read. I would show them a copy of the book from the pulpit and orders for the book would be taken through the office.

b. A series based on the prophets of Israel offered an opportunity to mark the steps in the development of the idea of God in the experience of Israel and to trace the roots of the ethical imperative in our heritage. Occasionally the responsive reading would be especially prepared from the words of the particular prophet under consideration.

c. Once a series on "The Dilemma of the Liberal" became the vehicle by means of which the concept of the liberal was projected and applied to various dimensions of our common life, our human relations, our religious experience.

d. When Sheldon Cheney's book *Men Who Have Walked with God* was published, it provided a wonderful combination of teaching and preaching in which I explained the significance of the inner life and the significance of piety in religious behavior. After such a sermon series the book itself was used as a text in a weekly study group for eight or nine weeks.

For a year or more we held a mid-week meeting at which the congregation was invited to listen to a recording of the Sunday sermon, at the end of which we had a full-scale discussion of the ideas. This gave the membership a chance to examine at close range the ideas that were being preached, and in the give and take between congregation and preacher new light was thrown on the meaning of some of the great concepts of religious experience.

Several times during the years I preached a series of sermons on the religious insights of certain Negro spirituals. Each Sunday during this series, the choir would sing the spiritual as an anthem. This series was brought to a full-orbed climax in a public lecture on the theme, given at one of the large Jewish synagogues in the city. This particular lecture was prepared and delivered as The Ingersoll Lecture on The Immortality of Man, at Harvard University, under the title "The Negro Spiritual Speaks of Life and Death."[1]

A very helpful method of preparing the congregation for the sermon was to select pertinent and concisely written themes in prose or poetry which I would read just before the sermon. This material always had in it the core of an idea concisely stated. It meant that if the congregation missed the idea in the sermon they would get a companion or correlative idea from the selection.

Also, each Sunday a special "meditation" printed on the back of the calendar, dealt with some basic idea which the worshiper could think of at his leisure. All of these aids helped to provide an increasingly rich and intelligent content for the feeling engendered by the worship experience.

The study groups had a like purpose but the procedure was different for obvious reasons. A study group met for a period of from eight to ten weeks, the minimum class time was an hour and a half. If a textbook was used it was made available to all who registered for the course. The first big undertaking was the use of Rufus Jones' *Studies in Mystical Religion,* which provided some understanding of the religion of the inner life and its influence in the lives of men and women who shaped the history of the church and the Christian movement. All of this made vivid the way in which the Christian revelation was at work in human history.

In the course of the year there were several study groups on the teachings of Jesus. One of the practical results of these courses was to challenge the mind to understand a little of what the Gospel stories of Jesus really say. This work was supplemented

---

[1] Published under the same title by Harper & Brothers.

The Letter and the Spirit

by one or two concentrated meetings on the Gospel records themselves.

A study group of a different kind was the use of Lecomte Du Noüy's *Human Destiny* as a text, and the book had to be read before the study group began. It is important to remark at this juncture that the listening to, and understanding of the Sunday sermon improved. Indeed it was exciting to sense the quality of anticipation and the heightened sense of awareness that made it possible for many people in the congregation to respond even to nuances of ideas. A fellowship of the mind became increasingly apparent. At the same time, the emotions were not left untended. We developed a counseling program.

One of the early problems in counseling was the fact that when certain illnesses occurred for which a psychiatrist was needed, there was resistance. Many people felt perfectly all right about going to a doctor about a physical ailment, but were apprehensive lest a stigma would be attached to them if they consulted a doctor about a mental illness. It was necessary then to see what could be done to help them accept the disciplines of psychology and psychiatry as resources for *healthful* living. A young adult club was organized, and one purpose of the club was to learn about mental health. Their first important project was a series of six Tuesday evening forum discussions, on the family, friendship, and the emotions. Through the courtesy of the Mental Health Society of San Francisco, six psychologists and psychiatrists acted as leaders of these forums. The program was not elaborate. A twenty-minute movie dealing with a particular problem was seen and then discussed under the guidance of the psychiatrist. Literature on the subject was made available, some of it for free distribution. The church library circulated the required books and prepared a suggested reading list. A series of sermons dealt with these problems by implication. The next subject for this group was an intensive study of the relationship of psychology and religion. It was limited to twenty-five people and the entire course cost one dollar. Each person was entitled to a thirty-minute personal conference. Once each year, for several years, there was some kind of conference on psychology and mental health. In due time, with many ups and downs, the adults learned to make use of the psychological disciplines for better health.

Before concluding this aspect of the story of Fellowship Church, something should be added about the place of prayer in the religious experience and training of the congregation. It needs to be remembered that a large percentage of the members of the church were persons who had had no previous adult experience with organized religion—except at weddings and funerals. And yet these members—and I say this parenthetically but emphatically—tended to be much more in tune with the concept of integration, which was a part of our ethical commitment, than those who had come into our fellowship from the segregated churches. On the other hand, they had almost no vocabulary and no working acquaintance with the basic religious concepts that were a part of the warp and woof of the church.

The emphasis upon prayer was built up very slowly. During the first year, I met certain individuals who seemed disciplined in prayer and who worked at it constantly. With several of them individually I entered into a kind of prayer pact. Sometimes when I had a particular concern, either personal or involving a need in the church or beyond, I would ask one or several to join me in prayer—each from his own place. There were no meetings together. It was a kind of anonymous prayer fellowship. I alone knew all the members of the group.

Then in the formal worship services prayer and meditation were never incidental. The period of pastoral prayer became more and more a time of guided meditation, silence, and therefore private praying. At length certain persons in the congregation became interested in meeting weekly at the church for meditation and prayer. This group has continued over the years but it has never been very large numerically; rather, it is like a prayer cell within the heart of the congregation. At times there were those who joined with them during the hour but remained in their own homes. This dimension of the religious life of the church was also strengthened by talks from the pulpit on the fundamental issues of communion with God. The body of the congregation as a whole, also, made good use of the printed meditations. It is my considered judgment that this was one of the most challenging aspects of our development, for I am certain that "more things are wrought by prayer than this world dreams of."

Even with the limited space in the church, there is a Meditation Room which is always available. The weekly meeting for prayer

The Letter and the Spirit

is held here. A description of the room was written by Jack Riley, a layman, who has been a part of this group from the beginning:

It is a simple meditation room in Fellowship Church. Nothing pretentious, just a quiet room where the brooding Spirit of God invades the silence.

On one wall hangs a painting of Gandhi by Howard Thurman. This saintly Hindu is leaning upon his staff, as he walks into a blazing aura of golden light. If one listens with his heart as he looks, he may hear Mahatma humming his favorite hymn: "Lead Kindly Light."

On a table nearby is a small statuette of Gautama whose thrilling struggle against the baser elements of self brought him from darkness into light. Here again, if one sees with the single eye, the Oneness of God, Tathagas' road, though different, is included.

Another table holds three books given to our Meditation Room by Congregation Emanu-El on the occasion of our Tenth Anniversary. Two are prayer books. The third is a beautiful book of etchings called *Pirke Aboth* (sayings of the fathers). All are written in both Hebrew and English. As one scans the pages of these books the significant contributions of Israel to the generations of men become apparent. The clarion call of the patriarchs seems to echo from the pages with the salutory invitation to prayer: "Hear, O Israel! The Lord our God is One."

In one corner, surrounded by growing plants, is a white statuette of peace sculptured by Preston Prescott. The spiritual quality of the face lends a calm serenity to the room. A book case contains books of our Judeo-Christian faith. What an experience it is to turn the pages and go on an imaginary walk with Jesus over the roads of Palestine. Or to be with him at the feast of the passover.

Occasionally someone asks: "How can all these different faiths worship together? How can they become reconciled when many denominations of the same faith cannot?" One analogous answer would be to liken God unto a diamond with many facets. No matter which facet one sees, the diamond is still a diamond. The Spirit of God may be revealed in many ways. Each is a facet of the truth or a facet of His Being.

As we worship God in silence, external layers of personality seem to fall away and the mechanics of the process become remote and irrelevant. As we move into the conscious awareness of the Irreducible Element of Self at our centers and identify with it, our consciousness expands until it becomes all-inclusive. Time stands still. The past and the future are wedded in the Now. There are no Christians, Jews, Buddhists, Moslems, or Hindus, as such, only children of God joined together in His Presence in a moment of high celebration. His all-pervading Spirit, moving at this level, transcends all mundane differences.

Each faith represented in the Meditation Room can be likened unto a beautifully pitched musical note. When all are blended together in the Presence of the Most High, they form a Harmonious Chord which might well be called a "Song of God."

Any person visiting our church during the early years would have been struck by the fact that there were few children present. There were few children because there were very few families in our membership. We knew that this situation would change. Would we be ready?

The future of any institution rests with its children. A movement constantly fulfills itself and redefines itself in those who come after. What were the implications of such a church as ours for parents? What was the meaning of our church for children? In what way can religion be taught to children? Or can it be taught? What should be the content of such instruction? Must it provide a frame of reference for the child that will equip him for dealing with the realities of his life or must it serve primarily as a point of referral for his life even though he may never be directly involved in it? These questions and many others are always being answered by the church and the answers are always being revised, restudied, and restated. Our experience was not unique except at one point. We were not operating out of a fixed pattern, which would have been true if we had been, for instance, a Presbyterian, a Methodist, a Baptist church.

Our first Sunday School was in operation before we moved out of the Fillmore district. This school was made up largely of Negro children from the neighborhood, with a few white children whose parents were teachers or volunteers in the church. When we moved out of the area, the composition of the school changed in due course. This created no problem in fact because the school was not a part of the life of the church.

The next important development was under the leadership of a young Japanese-American, Dave Tatsuno, who worked parttime with Fellowship Church and parttime in the employ of the Presbyterian Board where he was responsible for the rehabilitation of Japanese-Americans when they returned after the evacuation. Under his leadership, the Sunday School was largely Japanese-American with a few Caucasians and a few Negroes. But as soon as the Japanese-American churches were reopened as separate churches, our efforts in religious education were interrupted for the second time.

The third Sunday School was confined to one class which met before the morning service. I was the teacher. The children in attendance were the four or five whose parents were members of the church. Out of this beginning, a larger plan matured and as more parents became members, their children too became involved. The meetings were held for a while on Sunday morning before the regular church service. However, because we did not have a building to house our activities, we had to find other quarters that would be available on Sunday morning for religious education. For many months, such quarters were provided by the International Institute, but the work was poorly co-ordinated and almost without a plan. What was all-important, however, was that children were brought together under the guidance of certain adults who were committed to the ideals of the church.

When at last we were able to get the services of our first intern and his wife, we were on our way with a definite program. A committee of parents spent many hours discussing what it was they wanted to happen in religious instruction to, and for, their children. The great interest stimulated resulted in the church's first conference on the religious education of children. The importance of this conference and the discussions that followed cannot be overemphasized.

It was here that we were able to do careful thinking about our goals for the education of our children. At the core of our undertaking was the felt need for securing a climate which would serve as an incentive to worship God with directness and with simplicity. This goal involves a commitment of the life to God. It also involves a sense of worship that underscores the individual's private relation to God, a relation that is independent of any social, sectarian, or sex content. That is, our assumption is that in the worship of God the human spirit stands stripped of all the meaningful, but artificial, barriers that mark off one human being from another. In the presence of God we are not male or female, Methodist, Baptist, Unitarian, Catholic, or Buddhist; German, Italian, Swedish, or African—but human spirits laid bare without any of the pretensions by which, from day to day, we negotiate life.

The second goal was to develop a sense of participation in a process that would lead to the creation of a community of friendliness in which it will be reasonable for men to trust one another and to love one another. What we experience in the primary Fellowship, we seek to create and to implement in the wider community. This process is both social and psychological. It is social because it involves a cross-section of many human beings. It is psychological because it deals with the way the individual mind reaches out to make direct contact with other minds so as to give to itself a sense of community. We affirm that this sense of community is more insistent, more urgent, more compelling, than any concepts which separate one human being from another.

The third goal was to provide the tools with which people may make responsible, ethical, and moral decisions, that would enable them to reproduce, away from the Fellowship, the things which they discovered in the Fellowship. What are the tools? The first is Life! The individual must be glad just to be alive, even if he is having a hard time. This sense of being glad just to be alive is possible only if one believes in life—and if this belief in life is not initially or essentially moral. It isn't that he believes that life is good or bad; only that he believes that life *is*. The urge to be alive becomes one of the important expressions growing out of a commitment to God, and the commitment is the result of worship.

Our first job was to widen within ourselves the areas of aliveness. A man must seek to become alive to himself so that he will not seem to himself to be of no account. He discovers that he is neither good nor bad, but that he is both good and bad; that a part of the business of life is to expose more and more facets of his life to the scrutiny of God. This is the essential experience that a person seeks in the moment of worship.

He must also become alive to the world that is around him; alive to nature. The tendency is always to hold one's aliveness to the meaning of nature in check. If a man closely identifies himself with nature, he becomes afraid of doing some of the things that normally he wants to do. He may not eat meat or grain, for example, because he feels death very poignantly. This, interestingly enough, presents a paradox: as a man's aliveness increases in certain areas, it may also deaden in other areas.

He must become alive to other people. Often a person is afraid to bring all of his relationships to other people completely under the scrutiny of God. If he succeeds in so doing, it may upset all the other relationships that he has been building through the years. He begins to sense their needs; and as this happens, the only limitation that he can finally permit is the limitation in his ability to be a channel through which God meets their needs. The logic of this is suicide. If this danger is ignored, then a man becomes dead at spots where once he was alive.

How much aliveness with reference to others, then, may a person permit himself? As long as he tries to answer that question, he is safe. If, however, he deliberately keeps certain things away from the scrutiny of God, to that extent he is lost. He knows he can't fool God, but he thinks he is not responsible if he doesn't acknowledge it. When he discovers that aliveness in him is deeply involved in aliveness to others, then he must make the choice of being anemic, shriveled, undeveloped; or vital, enlarged, and less private.

One must also be alive to the holy Book. When a person studies the Bible, he discovers that he has no aliveness with reference to some parts of it. Again, he discovers that even within his Bible, which is within the total Bible, certain parts are especially significant to him, perhaps because they describe so accurately someone else, or because, to use the Quaker phrase, they speak "to his condition." He goes to them again and again, as a kind of rock that he reaches out to touch in the darkness. He can't see it and yet his hand knows what it touches.

An individual's Bible is not the holy Bible. He reads his Bible in his aliveness, with gratitude that it has meaning for him, and also with a great breadth of kindliness toward the God of the Universe because he has established other altar stairs that are foreign to his footsteps, up which men may climb to seek entrance into His Kingdom. This feeling is at first very difficult to encompass because of the sectarian character of Protestantism. But sooner or later one must be alive to other religions. It was stated earlier that in the presence of God the human spirit is naked, undisguised, and without pretense. Can a man believe profoundly in his own faith without establishing squatter's rights on other faiths? If it is true that the central act of the worship of God is the be-all and end-all of life, then can not such an experience in which the individual comes to an authentic understanding of his own personality and the meaning of life, be experienced anywhere, by anyone, without regard to the particular context out of which he comes? Can a man affirm this unity and at the same time walk with dignity within the context which is his?

One must also be alive to Jesus. Regarding Jesus, there is a mixed tradition in Christianity, a tradition that has two streams flowing down it. Sometimes they run along together, then break, then come back together. One is that Jesus is the divine moment in human life, that he is the word made flesh, that he is the incarnation of God; he is the great, dramatic "for instance" of the divine meaning; he is God; he is the illustration of how the infinite becomes finite; he is Redeemer and Savior. Around that concept has grown many ideas: ideas of his birth, ideas having to do with his complete mastery over nature, ideas of his mastery over death, ideas that have been cumulative in the history of the Christian movement and ideas which have appeared in creeds.

The other development is that Jesus was himself the subject of religious experience and that he, born out of the womb of Israel, felt that in himself the true meaning of Judaism blossomed and flowered. From birth to death he lived within the framework of Judaism. What he *did* with life, others can do—if they are willing to use the tools that are at hand. When that emphasis is given to Jesus, he becomes the source of inspiration and humiliation. Inspiration—because those who come after him have so much in him and make so little of it. In a man's confusion and frustration, it may be easier to worship Jesus than to walk in his steps.

In fine, religion has to be contagious. That is one of the glorious things about the moment of worship. Here is a parent who comes to church with her child; they sit together. Somewhere in the course of sixty minutes, when the songs are being sung, or when the mother's mind is gathered up into a collective, creative synthesis, the child senses her now not merely as his mother, but as a tremendous sharer in an experience of togetherness; he knows that his mother *is* his mother, as well as a member of the community. In the church school and the family, it is the experience of life with its overtone of value and meaning that will give a confidence in life to the growing child, so that as he grows up he will know that he can stand anything that life can do to him, and he is therefore free both to work and to make life free for all his fellows.

Over a period of many weeks, the teachers, the parents, and others discussed the various issues raised in our first conference, as we laid the foundation upon which the future of our work with children was built.

It is obvious that our handicaps were almost overwhelming. We were not a part of any denomination and therefore did not feel quite at home in the use of denominational literature available at that time. We felt somehow that we had to find an approach to religion and religious education that would give to growing children not only a sense of being at home in the world and a reverence for life, but also a sense of kinship with all children even though their features and their manners were unfamiliar, and their color different. In a sense our undertaking was doomed before it started because this point of view was not a part of the adult world in which the children lived, played, and studied. Very ambitiously we tried to create a curriculum that would spread our insights, but did not have the people with the training and the skill to do this effectively. Whatever we were able to accomplish was done by the devoted and intelligent lay committee of the church which met weekly to organize a curriculum.

When we moved to our own building in January, 1949, certain advantages were at once evident. Teachers and students alike could study and learn in the church building made sacred by the quality of the experiences which took place in it.

One of the most satisfying steps in this development was the Sunday morning family worship prior to the class instruction. A very simple worship altar was set up at the eye level of the smallest child seated in the smallest chair. Each class took turns in building the worship center. When the classes were studying the creation of the world, emphasizing the fact of God as the Creator of all things, it is obvious how such a theme would lend itself to pictorialization in a variety of altar settings. The constant elements on the altar were a lighted candle and an open Bible. The changing pictures varied from Sunday to Sunday: an arrangement of driftwood collected by the children along the shores of the Pacific, wild or domestic flowers, stuffed or toy animals such as squirrels, birds, and snakes. The committee worked out a plan of worship with an appropriate hymn, responses, and a simple prayer. I gave a five-minute worship talk. These programs were mimeographed and placed in booklets. The prayers, the hymns, and the responsive readings could be changed merely by taking the old ones out and putting new ones in. All of the children sat together. Some served as ushers and shared in the leadership of the service.

Always our effort was to relate our work in religious instruction to the life of the church. I was never unmindful of the possible pressure under which a child could be put by his peers because he was attending Sunday School at a church that was different or "queer." Constantly ways had to be found to surround the children with a deep sense of belonging to a fellowship of adults among whom were his parents. This would make for stability and confidence.

One of our teachers whose class was made up of a group of children from five to eight years old wrote a paper for us which she called "The Church School and Prayer." The immediate occasion for the experience depicted was the unexpected and lengthy illness of the Church School director. This is how she stated it:

> It is often difficult to put your point over with little children and particularly is this true if the subject deals in the abstract. To teach children to pray—how, when, and why we pray—has been one of the most crucial demands made upon the church school teacher, and particularly at the primary level. For how many of us, as children, prayed for the little red fire engine, or the big beautiful doll, only to find that our little desires weren't compatible with God's plan for us? Some of us are still asking, aren't we?
>
> The primary group in Fellowship Church School, ages five to eight, came face to face with prayer in human experience a few weeks ago when they were asked by their teacher to do something specific:
> "My dear children:
> "This is your Church School teacher again. It's quite a while since you had a letter from me, but your parents have had a lot to do, with the change of class time, the new choir, the new robes, the Easter flower presentation and the Easter Egg Hunt. Now that we're all settled again, we'll get back to a definite program. We have only one more story in our *Family Finds Out* and we'll do that Sunday after next. When we finish that story, we'll spend two Sundays talking about the book and what we liked and learned by knowing it.

"Next Sunday we'll have another story from *Teach Me To Pray* and I want you to see how many of the prayers you can remember and if you can remember 'How We Pray, Why We Pray, and When We Pray.' Also, if you remember any of the Bible verses we've learned to associate with praying. And tell us if you prefer to make up your own prayers.

"Now something special. As you know, our School Director is ill, and has had to go to the hospital. We sent him a get-well card last Sunday and this Sunday I'd like you to help me make up a very special one. This one will last a long time and will, I hope, make prayer a more personal thing for each of us.

"During the week before Easter, when he was probably very tired and not at all well, our Director conducted the Period of Renewal. They were beautiful services and I want to tell you something about them. He read to us from a French poet who wrote very beautiful religious poems. In one of them he tells us how God feels about little children saying their prayers. I have made a copy of part of it for you and I'll wait here while you read it!

"God speaks:

'As for me,' says God, 'I know nothing so beautiful in the whole world
As a mere child having a talk with the good Lord at the bottom of the garden;
Asking questions and giving the answers himself (it's safer that way,)
A little man telling the good Lord about his woes,
As seriously as anyone in the world,
And comforting himself as if the good Lord were comforting him,
But let me tell you that those words of comfort which he says to himself
Come straight and properly from me—
Nothing is so beautiful as a child going to sleep while he is saying his prayers, says God
I tell you nothing is so beautiful in the world—
And yet I have seen beautiful sights in the world.
And I know something about it. My creation is overflowing with beauty.
My creation overflows with marvels.' [1]

"Now, don't you think that was a pretty wonderful poem, and since this man was such a very holy man, don't you think he probably talked

---

[1] From "Innocence and Experience," by Charles Péguy, who was killed in action in World War I, August, 1914.

with God so much he really knew how God felt about the prayers of little children?

"I do.

"So, since the prayers of little children are so dear to God, wouldn't it be nice if each of you made up a very special prayer for our Director and told it to God each night, just before you went to sleep? And you might also say a little prayer just for his wife, so she won't be lonesome while her husband is in the hospital.

"I wish you'd each do that and write your prayer down on a small piece of paper and bring it to class. No one will read your prayer if you wish it that way, and we'll put them all together in the greeting card and mail it to him. If you wish to tell us about your prayer, that will be wonderful, but you don't have to! Don't forget to say the prayer each night (or whenever you pray) though, even if you haven't written it down.

"That's a pretty big order, I know. So, if you're fairly quiet (Dear Gilbert!) at the end of class I'll tell you an Indian legend about the 'Gift of Fire.'

"My love to all of you."

The prayers came in on the next Sunday, some folded in tiny, tight, little pieces for no eyes to see. Others brought in the prayer used to open and close class:

>God is with me now
>God is in me now
>God is the answer to my deepest need
>I possess myself in quietness and confidence.

The director was overwhelmed. "The prayers that the children sent me were very special," he wrote in acknowledgment. "Please tell them it meant a great deal to me knowing that I was in their prayers."

And they meant a great deal to little five- and eight-year olds, too, in their human experience of becoming aware of someone else's "deepest need."

The disadvantage of not being a part of a specific Protestant denomination gave us a decided handicap in our program of religious education. But it was an advantage to us in the experiments which we undertook in the general field of Worship through the Fine Arts. There were no theological windmills to battle, only the challenging task of getting the spiritual and psychological assent of the congregation. This involved overcoming initial resistance. Even in this we were helped by the fact that many of our congregation and membership had had very little previous adult experience in any church. There was certain openness toward religious experience even though the absence of an active religious vocabulary made communication slow, difficult, but sure and confident.

The Christmas Vesper service in December, 1943, was our first venture in the field of the fine arts. Unlike what we had presented at Howard University this was the presentation of a series of live Madonna types taken from the community and our congregation. With the assistance of Miss Annie Clo Watson of the International Institute we were able to select ten women—American Indian, Caucasian, Negro, Filipino, Korean, Chinese, Italian, French, and Armenian—who participated in the service. There was none of the elaborate equipment which I had used previously. Each face was framed like a picture and illumined by a soft light. The faces were viewed from the center of the stage and in pairs. Only one Ave Maria was sung—for the rest of the music the congregation sang carols. It was a community experience in which we were caught up and held. This is the prologue used for the occasion:

> During the season of Christmas in many art galleries, in countless homes and churches, and on myriad Christmas cards, there will be scenes picturing the Madonna and Child. There is a sense in which the Madonna and Child experience is not the exclusive possession of any faith or any race. This is not to gainsay, to underestimate, or to speak irreverently of the far-reaching significance of the Madonna in Christianity, particularly in Roman Catholicism. But it is to point out the fact that the Madonna and Child both in art and religion is a recognition of the universality of the experience of motherhood as an expression of the creative and redemptive principle of life. It affirms the constancy of the idea that life is dynamic and alive—that death as the final consummation of life is an illusion. The limitless resources of life are at the disposal of the creative impulse that fulfills itself most intimately and profoundly in the experience of the birth of a child. Here the mother becomes one with the moving energy of existence—in the dream of birth there is neither time, nor space, nor individuality, nor private personal existence—she is absorbed in a vast creative moment upon which the continuity of the race is dependent. The experience itself knows no race, no culture, no language—it is the trysting place of women and the Eternal.
>
> The Madonna and Child in Christianity is profoundly rooted in this

background of universality. Specifically, it dramatizes the birth of a Jewish baby, under unique circumstances, calling attention to a destiny in which the whole human race is involved. For many to whom he is the Savior of mankind, no claim as to his origin is too great or too lofty. Here is the culmination of a vast expectancy and the fulfillment of a desperate need. Through the ages the message of him whose coming is celebrated at Christmas time, says again and again through artists, through liturgy, through music, through the written and spoken word, through great devotion and heroic sacrifice, that the destiny of man on the earth is a good and common destiny—that however dark the moment or the days may be, the redemptive impulse of God is ever present in human life.

But there is something more. The Madonna and Child conception suggests that the growing edge of human life, the hope of every generation, is in the birth of the child. The stirring of the child in the womb is the perennial sign of man's attack on bigotry, blindness, prejudice, greed, hate, and all the host of diseases that make of man's life a nightmare and a holocaust.

The Birth of the Child in China, Japan, the Philippines, Russia, India, Africa, America, and all over the world, is the breathless moment like the stillness of absolute motion, when something new, fresh, whole, may be ushered into the nations that will be the rallying point for the whole human race to move in solid phalanx into the city of God, into the Kingdom of Heaven on the earth. . . .

Not only was the choir fundamental to our worship in the regular Sunday services but it was also our mainstay in what we were undertaking in Worship through the Fine Arts. Its resources were used as primary sources in the celebration of certain high moments in the Christian calendar, such as Christmas and Easter, and in special vespers. In addition to this, choral music was used throughout the year to amplify a religious theme by underplaying the hortatory use of the spoken word.

I discovered that it took a specific awareness and sensitive skill to keep the vesper music from being regarded as a recital or even as a sacred concert, by using a spoken prologue to establish the mood, announce the theme, and bring the congregation closer to the moment of encounter in worship. A definite form of pattern was used. Between the individual solo or choral numbers there were also spoken interludes—sometimes biblical, sometimes quotations from other appropriate materials. Even when a complete work was presented such as *The Ordering of Moses* by Dett, the same structure obtained—the work was surrounded by the

The Letter and the Spirit

spoken word to keep it geared to the intent and experience of our worship.

Another musical unit of worship was the handbell choir. Shortly after the end of the war, I was fortunate enough to get a famous handbell manufacturer in England to make a set of handbells for our church in San Francisco. The training of the group was in the hands of expert volunteer musicians. At one time the handbell choir was so proficient that they were able to carry an entire evening vesper program alone. Most of the music played were the great hymns. For these occasions the use of the spoken word was usually confined to the reading of majestic psalms. There were other times when the handbells provided a prologue for a particular choral vesper hour. This could be especially meaningful when the melody played by the bell ringers was one around which there centered many rich emotional overtones of worship. For important religious ceremonials the music of the bells was used in the call to worship. During the Christmas season special service was made of the bell ringers for reasons that are obvious. Their work eventually spilled over into the community with many visitations to hospitals, particularly children's hospitals, and to other institutions.

Some limited experimentation was made with the pictorial arts. They were employed in worship in a secondary sense and as an informal stimulation of the imagination. They were presented in the form of exhibits. Once, for instance, there was an exhibit of elegant prints of English cathedrals contributed by the Crosby family of Philadelphia. Another time, there was a formal exhibit of religious paintings borrowed from the community, which included a fairly large collection contributed by Peggy Strong, a nationally prominent artist who was a member of Fellowship Church. A unique experience with the pictorial arts was one in which roots from the High Sierras were used as the theme of a worship vesper. There is in the congregation a member, Cornelia Chase, who for many years has spent her summers in the mountains digging out the trunk roots of juniper trees. They are brought down to her studio in San Francisco and cleaned and polished by hand until their own luster shines forth. The shapes are studied and classified. It is easy for anyone with imagination to see what can result. These wood forms are used for many purposes, most of them decorative. The vesper service included an exhibit of these forms with appropriate prose and poetry readings having to do with the basic idea that the God of Life, the God of Nature, and the God of Religion is one and the same. When the vespers were over, individuals examined the root formations at their leisure during the tea or coffee hour, their appreciation noticeably heightened by the afterglow of the service. Many times during the year altar decorations composed of these wood formations graced the sanctuary of the church.

There was the gradual development of a verse-speaking choir. The principle of choric speech need not be labored. A number of voices, each true to certain quality and tonal registration, were joined into a vocal unit—a group made up of men and women of various ages. This group on occasion participated in the regular Sunday service, reading the Scripture or interpreting a specially selected responsive reading. On one memorable Sunday, the morning worship services proceeded as usual until the time for the sermon, which usually followed the meditation. Then, the verse-choir gave us excerpts from Hermann Hagedorn's "The Bomb Fell on America." The congregation responded unforgettably to the Spirit of God and the judgment of history. The minds of many were stampeded back to the fateful day not long previous when some of us sat with our Japanese-American secretary of the church as the terrifying tidings came over the air that an atomic bomb, for the first time in human history, had been dropped on a city—her native city. Many of her immediate family lived there. It was like a death watch.

The most radical of our ventures in the use of the fine arts was to incorporate the liturgical dance into the worship service. Radical to some, despite the fact that the role of the dance is well known in the long history of religion. It is the genius of the dance in its more literal aspects to effect by movement in space a creative synthesis of body, mind, and spirit. Modern man, too often beset by sins and anxiety, desperately needs experiences that make for wholeness, for synthesis, for validation. Our theory was that the liturgical dance would provide that kind of integrating moment.

The purpose of our liturgical dance choir from its formation in the fall of 1950 was to create complete dance services which would provide a worship experience both for the dancers and the congregation. During a period of three or four years, more than a dozen dance vesper services were shared by the congregation.

At first we were confronted with a real problem to find a way to introduce our congregation to the dance as a form worship. Certainly we did not want to further the notion that we were doing a thing simply because it was novel. One night at a dinner party in a friend's home I met a young man who had recently moved to San Francisco from the East and had opened a dance studio. After several months I went to see him in his studio to ask him to consider having one of his adult groups perform a liturgical dance vesper service at Fellowship Church. He demurred, saying that he knew little about the use of the dance as a form of worship. However, he was interested and invited me to come back at a later time to talk with his group; if they were interested, he would be glad to work with them.

In preparation for such a meeting I selected certain moods of the human spirit—moods such as joy, sorrow, contrition, faith, triumph. I found written material, poetry and prose, biblical and non-biblical, which was either descriptive of such moods or suggestive of them. The hour for the meeting arrived. As I look back upon it, I was quite excited and somewhat uneasy. The group and I were strangers. I presented my idea. There were many questions and much discussion. Finally I began reading the material I had brought with me. The first thing I read was from Tagore's "Gitanjali":

> When thou commandest me to sing it seems that my heart would break with pride; and I look to thy face, and tears come to my eyes.
>
> All that is harsh and dissonant in my life melts into one sweet harmony—and my adoration spreads wings like a glad bird on its flight across the sea.
>
> I know thou takest pleasure in my singing. I know that only as a singer I come before thy presence.
>
> I touch by the edge of the far spreading wing of my song thy feet which I could never aspire to reach.
>
> Drunk with the joy of singing I forget myself and call thee friend who art my lord.

Then a very extraordinary thing happened. Different members of the group began working out improvisations by applying their own dance disciplines and techniques to the mood, or more correctly, by letting the mood express itself through their dancing. The group was given the subjects and before the evening was over, all of the moods had been expressed by different members of the group, sometimes singly, sometimes in pairs. Just before the period was over, two dancers began working on something else. As we watched we knew that what they were doing was interpreting the meaning of worship. This at once became the prologue to the series. I did not visit the group again until advised that they were ready for the vesper service. Meanwhile, through the bulletin of the church, through many personal conversations, and by means of comments, sometimes from the pulpit, the congregation was prepared for the vesper and the response to the service was positive and healthy. After that evening we were ready to see if such a group could be developed from within our own congregation. Fortunately, there was a member, Lynn Buchanan, program director of the church, who had had extensive experience with the dance. It was he who undertook the development and the direction of the dance choir.

Our first completely original service was called "The Arc of the Day." The service began with a simple statement. "With words like windows to let the light through, a comtemporary poet leads the worshipers at day's end through a ritualistic design built upon the movement of the earth on its axis as it journeys through time and space." The dramatic instruments were a poet, a singer, a chorus of dancers, a fluid beam of light, a contemplative congregation, a choir of archaic instruments. As a prelude we listened to recordings of Gothic and Early Renaissance music played on ancient instruments—and we meditated.

The service had four divisions: the morning invocation, the noon meditation, the evening offertory, and the benediction. Here is a note on the first program: "With the exception of the poetry, the service is an original creation of the newly formed Liturgical Dance Choir of The Church for the Fellowship of All Peoples. Rhythmic and tonal effects are from music of the early church. Choreography, design of the robes, and certain ritual gestures have been abstracted from studies of early Christian church art. 'The Arc of the Day,' a direct expression of the immediate present, is thus also related to a distant time . . . to that period approximately a thousand years ago when the dance was still a vital part of Christian church worship."

The Letter and the Spirit   93

A kind of dance program different from "The Arc of the Day" was called "Meditation—A Liturgical Dance Vesper for the Quiet Time." As was our custom, we thoroughly discussed the concept and its possibilities with the individual dancers and with the choir as a whole. They decided that before they could fit the choreography to the theme it was essential for them to experience meditation itself. There were many discussions dealing with the meaning of meditation, its use, how it is related to prayer, and when it merges into prayer. During these discussions, individual members of the choir who had not been attending the thirty-minute meditation service on Sunday mornings decided that they needed this half hour of corporate worship for themselves. It was out of this experience that the architecture of the dance emerged. It was divided into three parts: on becoming still, on becoming centered, on becoming whole. A central figure, seated on a dais under a beam of light, remained throughout the dance. The dancers who were involved in the unfolding of the choreographic pattern moved in and out like shadows on the rim of the light in which the meditator sat. During much of the movement, meditations written especially for the occasion were read. The only music was a recording of a Chinese flute.

The choreography became a liturgy in movement. First there were the thoughts, in procession, representing the turmoil and the churning in the mind as the individual begins his journey into quiet. Slowly but surely some thoughts are examined, are stilled, are cast out, while others remain as a part of the struggle that goes on deep within the mind and the spirit of the individual. The movement for this section had to do with inner struggle, with what may be called in the language of religion, the war within the soul. The third section had in it all of the elements of wholeness, of integration, of quickening calm.

In the course of several years, the dance, which seemed at first to be some sort of innovation with an esoteric tinge, slowly became an integral part of the liturgy of the service. Some who first came to the church as members of the dance choir became members of the congregation of worshipers. Our persistent desire was to center on the use of movement as a litany of praise, of thanksgiving, of penitence, of illumination in the presence of God.

The use of the drama as a form of worship was slow to develop.

In several vesper services dramatic sketches were used as illustrations, and some effort was put into play reading, but the possibilities of the art as a form of worship were never realized. In all fairness, however, it should be said that a very significant contribution was made to the first Religious Arts Festival of the church when a group of young adults produced Sophocles' *Antigone*. Notwithstanding the fact that this play was given in the context of the Festival, there was a quality in its meaning that was centered in worship. This was due not only to the excellent performance but also to the climate of the Arts Festival in which it was produced.

That first Religious Arts Festival of the church, held in our fifth year, presented a program that lasted from Wednesday through Sunday. The English handbells provided a Prologue to the Festival, with six selections played on the stairway leading to the sanctuary, and then came the performance of *Antigone*. The next evening, the Liturgical Dance Choir gave a service called "Time, Place, and Impulse," a synthesis of the meaning of the dance vesper services during the year. On Friday, the singing choir presented Dett's *The Ordering of Moses*. On Saturday came the Festival party in which the entire congregation expressed joyful appreciation to all those who had participated in the Festival. On Sunday morning, a summary of the week was given in the sermon on the theme, "Art and the Religious Quest."

Through this series of successive, simple, and direct experiences of the fine arts used for worship there resulted a clearer understanding of the meaning of this aspect of the church's program and a deepening of everyone's quality of worship.

The work of the church became known not only through the regular journeys which I made to various sections of the country but also through occasional pieces of publicity in national organizations and by word of mouth. All of this in addition to the increasing number of members-at-large. More and more letters of inquiry and concern came to us. People wanted to know how we were faring. There was something more than curiosity or even good wishes—there was something wistful about many of my letters. What was clear from the beginning became increasingly urgent—we must find some way of reporting to those who did not live in San Francisco the success we were having and the problems we faced.

For the first year and a half, we mailed to our members-at-large an occasional mimeographed letter which gave a digest of past events, announcements of coming events, and a few paragraphs about certain facets of our commitment or some manifestations of religious insight. Then came the decision to prepare a more formal and ambitious periodical for local and national circulation.

Since the phrase "the growing edge" characterized the genius of the church itself, it was perfectly natural that when it was time to name the magazine, the choice of title should be *The Growing Edge*. At first it was a monthly, done by letter press, its contents in the format much like that of the occasional letters. Items included were a sermon that had been preached in the church, a meditation, some description of specific activities, and any other happenings of special merit we wanted our friends to know about. We were fortunate in having some friends in San Francisco willing to underwrite the cost of the publication for several issues in order to give it a chance to take hold. The subscription cost was gradually lowered from three dollars to one dollar. At first the resident members were asked to subscribe too, but soon we were able to send it to them free of charge. However, the monthly publication proved too costly and editorially too difficult to continue so it was decided to change to a quarterly.

When *The Growing Edge* became a quarterly, it was possible to publish a more ambitious periodical. In some issues two sermons appeared; one by the minister, and one by an outstanding visiting clergyman. In one issue we published the complete address given by Alan Paton when he visited the church and became one of its members-at-large. It was also possible to carry a few pictures of activities in which the church was involved. A report in *The Growing Edge* on an East Indian village food project sustained and supported by the church inspired many people outside of San Francisco to give it their support. Best of all, *The Growing Edge* kept interested people informed about the development of the life of the church and introduced many new people to the fact of its existence. However, to maintain the periodical was extremely difficult. We just did not have the funds at this time to give it the kind of publicity which in turn would have secured the number of subscribers needed to defray its operational expenses. From the beginning we realized that almost all journals of opinion have to be subsidized, and in our case many persons contributed to the limited subsidy we required.

At the beginning of the second year in the life of the church, it seemed appropriate to take advantage of the Christmas season by preparing for distribution a Fellowship Church Christmas card, which it was my privilege to write. Since we wanted a card whose text could be used to interpret some aspect of the purpose, the intent, the commitment of our church, use of the cards would mean that an increasing number of persons would be exposed to some of the ideas and ideals to which we were committed. During the past twelve years, more than one hundred thousand Christmas cards have been subscribed for all over the United States, and occasional orders have come from other countries.

With Miss Katherine Laux as its first chairman, an able committee of the church assumed total responsibility for their distribution, mimeographing an announcement giving the cost, the text, and a description of design, paper, and type used, packaging and mailing the orders. At the end of each season a financial report was prepared for the board. While the amounts realized were never staggering, they have been sufficient to augment the anticipated income of the church when the budget is drawn up. There is on file in the office a large collection of letters of comment that have come in a steady stream over the years.

In addition to Christmas cards, a few other cards have been distributed. A card bearing one of the meditations which appeared in *The Growing Edge* was designed and printed by an outstanding printer of San Francisco, Lawton Kennedy, as a contribution to the special dinner at which the church was celebrating its tenth anniversary. The text of this card, "The Dream in the Heart," synthesized the meaning of the Fellowship Church dream as our members—and so many others—identify themselves with it. One business firm in San Francisco ordered enough cards to give one to each of its key personnel.

A condolence card was published at this time for people who feel themselves unable to say the appropriate word in time of bereavement.

The involvement in seeking ever to find convincing experiences of spiritual unity as an attack upon old manifestations of separateness both for myself and our congregation had a profoundly stimulating effect upon my own mind. Until I came to San Francisco I had very little interest in writing. Under duress I had written previously a prose poetic interpretation of the 13th Chapter of I Corinthians and a longer poem on Jesus. But these were not published until my first year in San Francisco. As I moved more and more into the center of the process at the church I began feeling the urge to put into written form some of the things that were stirring within me. A very important part of my ministry was the weekly meditation written out of the heart of my own spiritual struggle and which appeared Sunday after Sunday in the weekly calendar. For several years I wrote a weekly meditation "working paper" for use by the congregation. Soon I was faced with the demand and the necessity for making collections of these available for wider distribution. The list of books grew, carrying into places I would never see the inner meaning of our adventure in faith and fellowship. Thus the written word became a very significant aid not only to us as a worshiping congregation but also as a means for a wider participation in the fundamental idea and an ideal upon which we had set our course.

While we were experimenting in many directions there was also emerging a definite organizational structure. In order to become incorporated under the laws of the State of California, we had to have a set of by-laws by which we were regulated. These established the broad outline of structure. Within this there was being developed the specific policies which gave body and the stability of continuity to our undertaking.

The spiritual leadership of our congregation was vested originally in two co-pastors of different ethnic or national backgrounds. This was deliberate: to put into the constitution of the church the formal intent to be an interracial congregation. That provision indicates one aspect of the self-consciousness of the venture. In order to appreciate the meaning of the provision, it must be remembered that the usual policy of a congregation seeking its leadership was here reversed: it was the minister or ministers who called on the congregation.

It took considerable invention to work out an arrangement whereby a co-pastorate could provide effective leadership to a young church for the basic reason that there is no pattern to which such an organization conforms. Since we were not a part of a denomination with an established polity and procedures we had to evolve a polity and procedure as we developed.

Dr. Fisk and I served as fully accredited co-pastors, but there were problems in this arrangement which both of us recognized. During this period, I devoted all of my energy to the church while Dr. Fisk continued as professor of philosophy at the San Francisco State College and could give only a part of his time to the church. Though more than a token co-pastorate, ours could never be conceived as a tested or actual one. This early arrangement, nevertheless, served two important purposes. The co-pastorate symbolized the kind of integration we wanted to obtain in all the church relationships of all the members. It was also a test of whether or not a community of fellowship within the congregation could be achieved that would offset the tendency to separateness which was the common experience of the members' lives in the workaday communities. It was crucial to discover whether or not there could be developed a bond of such authentic community that—contrary prevailing social patterns notwithstanding—the Caucasians would not gravitate to Dr. Fisk's leadership and the non-Caucasians to mine. The fact that this kind of gravitation did not take place gave the church, at its very inception, a spirit that sustained it through the many crises that were to come.

After Dr. Fisk resigned from responsible leadership in the church, I was the minister carrying final authority, the others serving as associates and assistants. This pattern of leadership continues to this day. My work as pastor was made easier by a dedicated board of trustees, the governing agent of the congregation having responsibility both for the fiscal and the religious nurture of the church. The board operated through a series of standing committees. The need for an officially scheduled business session called the entire congregation to one annual meeting. At this meeting new board members were elected, the budget was adopted, and all proposals having to do with policy or details of maintenance, or other items affecting the total life and wellbeing of the church, were ratified or rejected.

In the early days, the congregation was kept in intimate touch with the work of the board. Whenever necessary, special congregational meetings were called immediately following the mouring service. At first, efforts had been made to schedule such meetings at stated intervals during the week, but these were never effective. As the church program expanded, the distance, psychological and otherwise, between the board and the membership increased. We found a solution by using a San Francisco version of the New England town meeting, and as a matter of record we actually called our sessions "town meetings." At these meetings, there was full and free discussion, and recommendations were made to the board. Town meetings provided an excellent device for making the experience of the individuals in the fellowship available to the entire group.

During one particular period there was a general feeling that we were increasingly out of touch with our purpose. People were joining the church more rapidly and in larger numbers than could be assimilated. Signs of segmentation began emerging —there were those who felt advantaged by virtue of a larger membership in the church. Evidences of unrest were unmistakeable. I suggested that we take a long careful honest look at ourselves. This was done by scheduling a series of small town meetings to be held in the homes of the membership on a sectional basis. Those persons who lived in Berkeley and Oakland met in a group in that area and those down the peninsula met in a group in that area and so on until the entire membership had the opportunity of involvement. With the help of persons trained in group discussion techniques, groups throughout the membership thus discussed matters that needed to be brought up at the scheduled town meeting of the congregation as a whole. At the big meeting, the entire group was informed of whatever had taken place in each of the smaller discussion groups. All matters affecting the church, including its leadership, came under careful scrutiny. It was a sober and enlightening experience for the minister to sit through a town meeting and hear what the congregation had to say about his sermons and his other services as pastor. The net result of all this was a quality of experience healthy for the congregation and for the future of the church. Out of it came a way of dealing with any crisis that would allow the time needed for full discussion.

For five years the church enjoyed the leadership of the very gifted program director, Lynn Buchanan, whose ability provided some of the skills for implementing many of the unusual ideas which found their way into the function of the church. Below is a sample of the working diagram of the church for 1953.

Very early in the organization of the church, the idea of providing opportunities for first hand experience for young men entering the ministry seemed consistent with our purpose. The experience in Fellowship Church would provide the young men with a chance to work with people of different backgrounds and cultures, united in a common religious commitment. From face-to-face meetings with our congregation they could learn much that would help them in their future ministries to work always for inclusiveness.

The original idea was to have an intern from a different denomination for each twelve-month period. First, of course, it was necessary for the church itself to find a way to finance such an internship. In the very nature of our operation the struggle for funds was grim and real, and this move meant the church's taking upon itself additional financial burden for extra leadership which it did not really need. The congregation had to be convinced of the wisdom of such a program. The expenses for the first intern were $2500. We were able to secure $1500 of this amount from friends interested in the idea and its implications for Christian leadership. Then one hundred people in the membership contributed $10 each which guaranteed the total needed. Before the intern was chosen the $2500 was secure.

Our first intern, Robert Meyner, was a member of the Congregational Church and during his internship with us he was ordained by the Congregational Association. At the end of the first year, I was invited to serve as a visiting professor at the University of Iowa for the winter semester. Upon the recommendation of the board, the congregation invited this intern to stay a second year and to serve as assistant minister. In this capacity he carried the major leadership responsibility for the church during the period of my intermittent absence, for I returned to San Francisco about every six weeks.

As we approached the end of the second year, the significance of the internship had the support of the congregation. Thus we were able to look for someone else, preferably from another denomination. We held preliminary conversations with several denominational leaders and decided on a plan in which the denomination would pay the salary of the intern and Fellowship

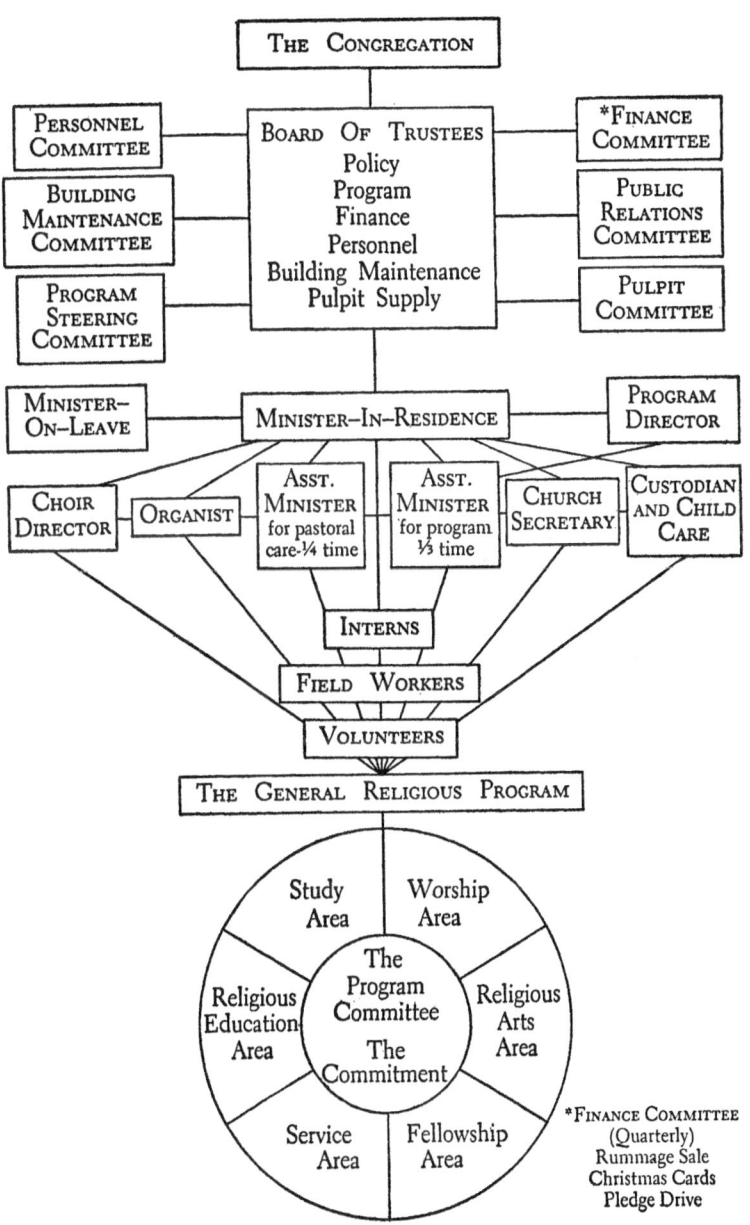

Church would provide supervised training and a place to live. One denominational leader so believed in the possibility of the plan that he and I began considering some young men from his church, and such a man was invited from the East. Before the arrangement could be completed, however, we learned that from within the denomination there was not enough backing to support its share of the plan. When we had almost given up the possibility of finding someone, the executive secretary of the American Unitarian Association, the late Dr. Frederick May Eliot, was able to co-operate to the extent of recommending a young man, James Brewer, from his church and guaranteeing his salary for twelve months. It may be noted that he is now the minister of the Unitarian Church of Norfolk, Virginia, where daily he finds that his experience with Fellowship Church provides a unique wisdom for his work as the spiritual leader of a liberal congregation in a Southern community.

The present minister, Francis Geddes, served two summers as an intern prior to his graduation from the Yale Divinity School. After his graduation, the church invited him to join the staff as an assistant minister, carrying specific responsibility for religious education and certain other aspects of the program. He served in this capacity for almost a year, and some three years later he returned to the church as its full-time minister. Under the leadership of Geddes, emphasis is being placed on this dimension of service which the church can render to the ecumenical movement. Under his guidance a fund has been established, to which many persons within and without the congregation have contributed, the purpose of which is to provide opportunities for young people to share in the life of the church in the summer, men who are theological students in some other part of the country, as well as to provide one full-time internship covering the period of a year. This means that within the next ten years it may be possible for as many as fifteen young men, some of them married, to have a firsthand experience living and working and learning within the fellowship of the church. This will give them confidence in the practicability of developing a religious fellowship across all lines of race and culture without regard to denominational affiliation. These men will come from many denominations.

For two years, the church had the rare experience of having

a woman, Miss Adena Joy, serve as the assistant minister. What was so rare was not the fact that she shared in the religious leadership of the church, but that she carried some of the responsibility in the pulpit as the preacher during the periods of the absence of the minister.

In addition to these interns, students from a neighboring theological seminary, The Pacific School of Religion, worked as student assistants in various capacities. All of this meant that during the first ten years more than a dozen persons who have subsequently become professional workers in regular churches were acquainted with the problems and the significance of Fellowship Church. It is difficult to overestimate the far-reaching effect these people will have on the future of American Christianity.

From the very beginning various individuals who were interested in the idea behind our experiment contributed financially as an earnest of their belief in the church's future. The first sustaining support came from the Presbyterian Church, U.S.A. through their Board of Church Extension. Soon, however, the church became financially independent of any group or denomination. Contributions came in from members-at-large in different parts of the United States. Certain schools and colleges contributed modest sums from their campus organizations. Many San Francisco friends of the idea made annual contributions.

The budget was divided into two main parts: There was the division which had to do with the operation of the church and the maintenance of the public worship of God. The ministers and the board decided that the resident members should carry the primary responsibility for financing this part of the budget and the congregation did so, magnificently.

The second division of the budget came under the general heading of special projects. It was thought that a small congregation such as ours could not be expected to finance experiments to further the idea on which we were working. Such experiments as the Intercultural Workshop, the dance choir, the internships, and the magazine *The Growing Edge* were in whole or in part, underwritten by persons or groups interested in the particular experiment.

There was nothing more inspiring in these early years than the spirit with which so many of these contributions were made. One woman from a distant city attending a professional meeting in San Francisco came to worship on a Sunday and later became a member-at-large. Because of her religious experience on that particular Sunday, she found herself free of a deep anxiety which she felt about a serious surgical operation she had to undergo a few weeks after the visit. Her gratitude to God for the insight and reassurance which came to her on that day is expressed by an annual contribution to the church made on each anniversary of that visit. Another woman sent a note saying that she would make her winter coat last one more year so that she could contribute to the work of the church. A group of girls in a preparatory school in the East contributed twenty children's chairs for the Intercultural Workshop. Each year, a substantial percentage of the total budget of the church came directly from individuals and groups over the country with whom I had shared the contagion of the dream.

Sometimes the equivalent of money was given to develop the work. A local Presbyterian church gave the hymnals that the original group used during the first six months of worship together. The First Unitarian Church of Germantown, Pennsylvania, gave one hundred and fifty hymnals and later another hundred, all of which are still being used in the church. Several members of the Hennepen Avenue Methodist Church of Minneapolis visited the church and were so inspired by their experience of fellowship that largely through them we were able to secure half of the salary of a young man who was to devote all of his time to the religious education program.

It was my custom to give to the church any honorariums I received for lectures or preaching either locally or anywhere on the West Coast. Certain very important contributions were made by groups of churches into whose leadership I was invited for some special purpose. For instance, a group of downtown churches in Portland, Oregon, invited me to conduct a Preaching Mission for a week. I made, and they accepted, this proposal: I would speak twice a day for five days and once on Sunday if they would agree to contribute $1000 to Fellowship Church's program. Another time I conducted a three-day institute for the board of the YWCA of Long Beach, California, on condition that they would levy a registration fee of $2.50 for each person who attended—the check being paid to Fellowship Church for its work.

It is only fair to say that our small congregation could not possibly have financed the kind of program we developed, and despite all the help which came from friends, members-at-large, and the local congregation, we were constantly on the razor's edge of financial insolvency. We never resorted to the usual devices of suppers and the like for raising funds. Always we wanted people first to identify themselves with the cause, and then, because they believed, to give their support. With this stipulation, funds could never be solicited in the ordinary way. This part of my task was primarily educational. There were times when we had to refuse funds because the persons who offered them were indifferent to the idea or the commitment but wanted to use the contribution as means to ends that we could not sanction.

All through the first years we were without a church building, and had to move our place of worship three times in four years. In January, 1949, we had the chance to buy a church building owned by an Evangelical and Reform congregation. One Sunday morning, after we had been worshiping there for some time, Miss Hulda Niebuhr, the sister of Dr. Reinhold Niebuhr, was present in the congregation. During the coffee hour after the service she was introduced to the group and made a most moving statement which will be remembered always by all who were present. Her remarks were concerned with the Evangelical and Reform congregation that owned the building in which her father preached many years before. He was even then concerned with bringing people of European and of American backgrounds within the context of the Christian commitment, to experience fellowship together, the very concern which, many years after, was a part of the guiding idea of this new small Fellowship Church. At that earlier period his idea was most effective and fulfilled itself in the Evangelical and Reform congregation, the descendants of whom sold us the building. Thus, in us, another man's dream was finding fulfillment.

But to return to the purchase of our first church. The cost of the property was $30,000, with an additional $6000 needed for repairs and refurbishings. A notation from the minutes of the meeting of the board at which the decision was made reads, "The treasurer's report announced the new deficit for the month as $275. It was then unanimously voted to buy the new church." The board recommended its decision to the congregation at the following Sunday congregational meeting, and its recommendation was approved. One member of the congregation, who at that time was not a member of the church, was so convinced in that meeting that she made an anonymous contribution of a $500 bond to the new church, which bond she had inherited many years before from her brother. It is impossible to overestimate the effect of that kind of untutored enthusiasm on those of us who were carrying the daring responsibility of trying to raise $30,000 while we still barely kept alive by deficit financing.

We tapped every available resource in the community to see if a loan could be negotiated. Certain property owners in the church and other responsible persons were willing to be joint signers of a note, but such a proposition was not acceptable to any financial institution. We had one conference with an institution in which there seemed to have been an initial interest in making the loan. The committee was carefully examined—about the church, its aim, its backing, its type of membership. As it was slowly revealed what kind of church we were, we were told that it would be difficult enough to make a loan to us if we were a regular church, a part of a historical denomination. But such a church as ours could not survive in American life and therefore under any circumstances we would be a bad risk.

Without seeming overpious, it is certainly true that our spirits were steadied and inspired by what to us was the movement of the Spirit of God in our midst. We were required to pay cash for the building. The loan was made from a fund established by a family in another part of the state. Individual members of the family had for some time maintained a committed interest in the development of the church. We were able to secure this loan without interest for three years, under the agreement that we would amortize the loan at $10,000 a year. The board, under the leadership of its chairman, Gene K. Walker, assumed this responsibility. The funds were raised through a national committee of which Arthur Crosby was chairman. In three years the entire loan was repaid, and at a high moment on a Sunday in January, 1952, the mortgage was burned in a special ceremonial. Here is the account of the ceremony as it appeared in the issue of *The Growing Edge* for the spring of 1952.

The small sanctuary was filled. As usual, folding chairs in the back took care of those extras who were not politely asked to go downstairs and listen to the service through the speaker system in Fellowship

Hall. From the south the warm sun came through the stained-glass windows—windows distinguished not by beauty, but by the large areas of unpatterned glass that let in the light. The rays of sunlight made pallid the white candles flickering in the standing candelabra and heightened the beauty of the flowers in a large bowl, centered on the platform back of which rose the brown wooden partition screening from view the choir director and organist. The warm flow of the noonday sun had its response in the warm tones of the choir, in the warm chorusing of the congregation as all united in a familiar hymn.

The gently formulated rituals of another Sunday service at Fellowship Church had begun. But this Sunday the pattern gave way to a special ceremony. The congregation was aware that standing in the central aisle below the rostrum were three men. The one in the rear ceremoniously held a brass tray. Significant words, spoken reverently, thoughtfully, and the man with the brass tray, conscious of the drama of his part, stood gravely immobile. A touch of light and the mortgage burst into flame.

The light of love and affirmation filled the unpretentious box-shaped sanctuary, with its solidly beamed ceiling, its plain benches, its chair-filled choir loft, while the sun streamed through the stained-glass windows, its family-like congregation involved in a moment of high significance. The burst of flame turned to ashes; the choir chanted a rhythmic folk melody. And as the congregants resumed their seats, after reading in unison the commitment "I affirm my need . . ." Dr. Thurman began:

"I would like to take a few minutes to interpret the meaning of this experience. . . . The social structure, the economic order, the world of nature, all of these apparently mindless forces in the world, repeat one theme over and over—THIS IS A UNIVERSE! THIS IS A UNIVERSE! Over and over! Only man says it isn't. And he builds his little shelter; raises his little wall; builds his little altar; worships his little God; organizes the resources of his little life to defend his little barrier. AND HE CAN'T DO IT!

"It is our faith that in the presence of God—with His dream of order—there is neither male nor female; white nor black, Gentile nor Jew; Protestant nor Catholic; Hindu nor Buddhist nor Moslem—but a human spirit, stripped to the literal substance of ITSELF! And wherever man has the scent of the Eternal Unity in his spirit, he hunts for it! In his home, in his work, among his friends, in his pleasures, on all levels of his functioning . . ."

And that is why Fellowship Church is a normal church, not an abnormal one . . . and what a wonderful thing it is to anticipate the future—in the present!

This was an experience of confirmation. Here were five hundred people, Jew and Gentile, black and white, rich and poor, clergy and lay, men and women, youth and age, sharing a spiritual unity in celebration of a concrete religious fellowship that in its daily functioning demonstrated that experiences of community are more compelling than all the things that divide.

One friend, a factory worker in New York City, sent a letter for the occasion. In this letter she said, "I am unable to make the kind of contribution that will mean very much in the liquidation of so large a debt, but I am enclosing what I can, a dollar bill. Will you use it to keep the hinges greased so that those who come in and out can do so with ease."

At a dinner held in one of the large dining rooms of Riverside Church, a committee of citizens of New York City, under the chairmanship of Dr. Channing H. Tobias, presented the minister of Fellowship Church and the chairman of the board, and then gave them a purse of more than $2500 for the program of the church. Many of the persons who were present at the dinner were members-at-large. For the occasion, one couple came to New York City from as far away as Toronto.

4. The Image of the Church

IT WAS NOT MERELY the fact that our church was deliberately organized as an interracial church that made the experience of membership, as of internship, unique and valuable both in the present and for the future. But rather, the fact that in the very nature of the case we had attracted an exceptionally heterogeneous membership and congregation. Until as recently as 1953 the "racial" breakdown in percentage was approximately 60 per cent Caucasian and 40 per cent non-Caucasian. Of the non-Caucasian percentage, 35 percent was Negro and 5 per cent non-Negro. Because the climate of America favors racial separateness, up to the present time very little is known about what conditions are necessary to maintain a racially integrated organization that is at the same time completely permissive as to membership. Constantly I was trying to find some clue to the fact that our membership did not conform to the pattern but remained consistently integrated. When the leadership of the church changed, the percentages were reversed and up to the present time there is no real insight as to cause and effect in this matter.

In addition to racial and cultural heterogeneity we were a cross section of the urban community in another way. There were not many professional people aside from a few public school teachers, office secretaries, nurses—one dentist, one lawyer, and an occasional businessman. Of the several academic institutions in the Bay Area, we had only three faculty persons represented in our membership. By the end of the first three years these had withdrawn. We were not a "workers" church nor were we a "white-collar" church.

The simplest way to describe the membership is to let a sampling speak for itself. As a part of the transition from my active leadership of the church to someone else's, a committee of twenty-five persons was selected from the membership, including some members of the board, to make a study of the membership. One of their aims was to examine the image of the church in the minds of its members. This was undertaken by means of a short questionnaire. Here is a sampling of the replies to the two questions relevant to this story:

What do I expect Fellowship Church to do for me?
What do I expect Fellowship Church to do for others?

WHAT DO I EXPECT FELLOWSHIP CHURCH TO DO FOR ME?

... I expect Fellowship Church to serve as an instrument which will liberate the divine in me and all others. Besides the Church being an assembly for thanksgiving to God, I want its viewpoint to be disciplined and I want it to demand of me and others knowledge of my Christian heritage. I want Fellowship Church also to enrich my life with the wisdom of the many great religious viewpoints in the world.

... I expect my church to make an attempt to find out the reason for my absence from church should this occur. We at Fellowship Church have often thought of those who possibly, after regular attendance, might happen to be away from Fellowship for several Sundays, but I wonder how many of us have attempted to find out why that person has been absent. It is that certain personal touch that often decides whether an individual maintains his relationship with an organization or even with another individual. We all like the feeling of being missed or needed, and when someone drops us a card saying that we have been missed, the feeling of discarding many of the things responsible for our absence is created.

... I expect from Fellowship Church a satisfaction of my spiritual needs which I expect it to provide for others.

... My church should provide me with sanctuary; a place where I may come and find this sanctuary either in quiet meditation, dynamic spiritual inspiration, or in noisy social activity. My church should provide for me an island on which I may find spiritual inspiration—spiritual challenge; a group recognition of individual human dignity and decency; and the chance to work for a dream.

... I look to my church for the provision of a climate which is conducive to worship ... a sanctuary to which I may repair at any and all times for prayer, for meditation and for spiritual counsel and guidance; where I may hope to be enlightened concerning my relation and obligation to God, to my contemporaries, to posterity and to myself.

... It is difficult for me to separate what I would want Fellowship Church to be for me from what I would want it to be for others. I prefer to think in terms of what I want it to be for everyone. I think that first of all it should be a place of worship. Secondly, I think it should be a place where men may come together to share in the search for a better understanding of God, and through Him of each other, and of all men everywhere—a place where men may grow together in wisdom and maturity, seeking for the enrichment of their own lives and for valid principles of action for the solution of human problems on a broader scale.

. . . I should like for Fellowship Church to continue to mean what it has meant to me for the past ten years—a sanctuary for worship and meditation with others who seek a growing understanding of God and man . . . fellowship in the experience of spiritual growth by serving with others dedicated to the working out of God's purposes . . . and warm, personal friendships which have so enriched my everyday living.

. . . I expect my Church to present to me a spiritual challenge to point a way for me to seek after a greater spiritual understanding. At Fellowship Church I have an opportunity to share my views with people who have similar aspirations, to gain an understanding of all men as sons of God.

WHAT DO I EXPECT FELLOWSHIP CHURCH TO DO FOR OTHERS?

. . . In recognition of the love which binds us together and of the mutual entertainment of common goals and ideals, I believe that wherever practical such channels of communication should be serviced by devices such as *The Growing Edge*.

. . . I expect Fellowship Church to do for others what it does for me; that with this basic, cardinal, religious foundation, it will share with others the love, understanding, and universality of God.

. . . I want this to be a place where all growing children can feel a sense of being wanted, of belonging, of finding someone who is interested enough to listen to them; work with them and help them (outside of and supplementary to the home) find their own unique place in the world.

In reading over these replies I was again impressed with the seriousness with which they were considered. The replies to the questionnaire were used as the basis for a series of town meetings of the congregation out of which came certain definite recommendations and decisions looking toward the future.

To prepare for the writing of this story, I felt that it was important to take a look at the motives which prompted people to join the church in the first place and the difference that their joining has made in their attitudes toward other people. I recognized the precarious character of this undertaking, but I was eager to get some picture of the member's image of himself in relation to the church. Many members hesitated to commit to writing their reactions because it seemed to them, and rightly so, to be a sharing of one's private life for public scrutiny. There were others who felt that to call attention to such intimate experiences would be to introduce an element of unreality and self-consciousness in their subsequent behavior. One of our most persistent insistences, from the beginning, was the recognition of the peril inherent in our experience in the church if we regarded it as abnormal. The threat of social exhibitionism rested uneasily on the threshold of our undertaking. In the language of religion, this threat may be defined as pride and self-righteousness, the twin malignancies of spiritual growth. All of the misgivings felt by the members were honored. Of the reactions sent in, the following is a fair and adequate sampling of the answers to

Why did I join Fellowship Church?

What difference, if any, has the church made in my attitude toward people?—In their attitude toward me?

Have I had any experience that tested my loyalty to the commitment?

Have I observed any effect of the church on the community or persons who encounter it for the first time?

WHY DID I JOIN FELLOWSHIP CHURCH?

... because I wanted to worship God in a church that is open to all people without regard to race, creed, or culture. Having been born in the South of Quaker heritage, I had a conflict of emotions resulting from the racial prejudice that surrounded us, and from earliest childhood the unfairness, that was considered fair, practiced toward colored people, was of deep concern to me. When I found a church where people gathered with a dedication to seek God and know each other with spiritual concern first, I felt a sense of "home-coming" unknown before, and I joined forthwith.

... Two years ago when June and I were privileged to work on the Fellowship Church staff as summer interns, I experienced a relationship with my fellow man that I had only dreamed possible before. We had accepted the opportunity to go to San Francisco from the Boston University School of Theology because we believed we had found a church which was truly presenting a witness to mankind—a witness we felt was the vital message that Jesus of Nazareth delivered in his time. June and I believed the Commitment of Fellowship Church before going, only to find it becoming fulfilled in the experience of devoted members of the fellowship. As we became involved in the Tenth Anniversary celebration, the renovation work, and the regular program of the church, we began to discuss our relationship with Fellowship Church. Before we left to return to our educational work, we realized that we, too, were involved in the witness of this fellowship of all peoples. We realized that from this point on in our lives, "things would be different." We would try, more creatively, to live more fully our dedication and commitment to God. Fellowship Church had given us new perspective through the sharing experience. This sharing experience would not be complete unless we left San Francisco to continue our task as members-at-large, with the hope that what had been given to us through Fellowship Church might be returned in some small particle through a continued relationship. Perhaps this is not the why, but it suggests the tremendous sharing experience which led me to join Fellowship Church.

... because I believe in what it stands for, that there should be no racial barriers.

... because I felt the need for spiritual growth; but I had no religious dogma. As St. Augustine said, "my soul was restless" and I hungered for an experience of God, but churches such as I had attended did not feed this hunger.

... I joined Fellowship Church because it satisfies an intellectual as well as a spiritual need.

... for seven weeks I enjoyed the fellowship and friendship of the fine people of that church and very reluctantly I said farewell. But I signed the register before I left for Canada and am proud to be a member there, to signify how much I am in accord with the work of that remarkable church, to support its work by my prayers and means.

... I joined Fellowship Church because the Commitment reaffirms my belief in the "oneness" of people and the "oneness" of religious faiths.

... Since I seemed to be there, listening to the heartbeat and pulse of Fellowship Church before it was born, perhaps I cannot really say why I joined—but I do know that Fellowship Church joined me. It was fifteen years before that I had left my home church when the minister told me I could not teach the children because I found myself unable to "believe" a certain part of a creed. This experience left a deep impression on me since I interpreted it to mean that my participation in church life could only be at the cost of my personal religious integrity. Fellowship Church said to me and continues to say, "Come, let us worship God together, each in his own way."

WHAT DIFFERENCE, IF ANY, HAS THE CHURCH MADE IN MY ATTITUDE TOWARD PEOPLE—IN THEIR ATTITUDE TOWARD ME?

... before joining the church, I would qualify people by their religious or racial heritage as "my Jewish friend, Negro, Oriental, Roman Catholic," etc. Now I seldom have the impulse, my friends are my friends!

... some of the members of my former church are puzzled.

... My parents had no race prejudice—so neither did I. With what Christian understanding I possessed it seemed incongruous to me that we could seek God and not love all His people. I did not have an opportunity to make friends with those other than the white race. Through Fellowship Church, I now do and it has greatly enriched my life. Though I always knew that people shared the same moral, spiritual, and intellectual life regardless of race or creed, I may have been color conscious, where now I am unconscious of color. I now am like the little white boy whose mother asked him if Jimmie, with whom he played at school, was a little white boy or a little black boy. The boy said, "I really don't know, mother, but tomorrow I will look and see."

... The difference the church has made in my attitude toward people is to increase my confidence in "oneness" because of the perfectly natural fellowship expressed by those of widely different backgrounds working together toward a goal of universal love and an integration of differing religious faiths.

HAVE I HAD EXPERIENCE THAT TESTED MY LOYALTY TO THE COMMITMENT?

... When I was preparing to lease my home for a year, I made an effort to find tenants from one of the minority groups. I was disappointed to be unsuccessful, but felt the expressed desire may have had some constructive effect through calling a number of real estate firms and having them realize that there are people who want to share their homes with all people. I have stopped dealing with a dress shop that has very good merchandise because they refuse to sell to Negroes.

... I used to find it more comfortable to keep still when race prejudice came into the conversation. Now I am usually uncomfortable if I keep silent. However, I find at times it is wiser to keep still and other times it seems wiser to give my opinion. For example, neighbors were in our apartment and mentioned with apprehension their fear of Negroes moving into the neighborhood. The wife, in particular, was greatly agitated. She expressed herself vehemently and my husband and I kept very, very still. In a few weeks we were in their home and the subject came up again, but this time I spoke my little piece and I believe the "vaccination" took. At least they know just where we stand and I am sure it will influence their thinking. Though I am not sure of any religious dogma and do not know what parts of the Bible should be interpreted literally, or otherwise, I do know I am right in my belief on the equality of man regardless of color, and feel it so deeply that no church could satisfy my searching as does Fellowship Church.

. . . When it comes to "oneness" of religions, I have to take my stand even in Fellowship Church, on the interpretation of the Commitment, whether we are a Christian church tolerant of other faiths or whether we are a church of predominantly Christian orientation who understand and accept the common values in all faiths. I stand for the latter view.

HAVE I OBSERVED ANY EFFECT OF THE CHURCH ON THE COMMUNITY OR PERSONS WHO ENCOUNTER IT FOR THE FIRST TIME?

. . . I think the church has already made an effect on the community when we are asked to allow our sanctuary to be used for a play about Roger Williams by the Actor's Workshop. Also, the refusal to sign the Loyalty Oath is evidence of our desire to live up to our commitment.

. . . we found a new perspective in our married life together.

. . . Among strangers there is a glow.

. . . the church has definitely helped in racial understanding.

. . . The effect on the community or on the persons who encounter our church is inevitably good. Though some may come the first time through curiosity, when they hear such men as Dr. Thurman, the Rev. Mr. Geddes, our fine guest speakers—all with inspiring messages —and they hear a choir of outstanding voices, see people of various races sharing the hymnals, singing together, visiting congenially after church, they can't help being impressed. . . . We find people are interested in what we are doing.

. . . Persons coming to Fellowship Church for the first time, when greeted, are often so interested in what they heard and saw that they sign the Visitor's Guest Book and ask if they may receive more information concerning the program of the church.

. . . As a member of the Hospitality Committee and then the Membership Committee, I have had the opportunity to get the reactions of a good many visitors, both local and from all around the world— which means that news of what we are trying to do brings all these people to the church. The visitors are very pleased with the service. They are glad they came and want to come again, and many want to be on the mailing list.

. . . A young woman, who broke away from a strict orthodox Jewish background, came to Fellowship Church out of curiosity. She came again and supported the church in many ways, although she never joined. Summarizing her experience, she said, "I can find many groups which are tolerant of various races, but this is the first I have found which is tolerant of religion."

Members-at-large maintain, of necessity, an informal relationship to the church. It is never quite possible to involve them in the overall activity of the church in a consistently creative and effective manner. They are kept informed of the program through bulletins, and finally through *The Growing Edge*. The weekly Sunday calendar and other materials of the church are mailed to them. When I, as minister, made annual visits to different parts of the country, informal meetings were scheduled with these groups in certain places and a progress report made. But there is never enough time or imagination to spare from the local development to devise an organizational technique that would tie them together as an active part of our corporate fellowship. In spite of this, they are a vital part of our communion and their relationship even at long range produced important results: Many of the members-at-large include in their vacation trips to the West each year a visit to San Francisco to be with the church in its worship and program. Many of them interest their friends in visiting the church when they can come to San Francisco. Each one of these first visits helps to kindle in them confidence in the practical possibility of our kind of fellowship in their own communities. Through members-at-large word about the church is circulated nationally and internationally and thus inspires many dreams and hopes.

I remember being on a train between Champaign, Illinois, and Chicago when a man walked slowly by my seat, then turned around and came back. He asked if I were not the minister of The Church for the Fellowship of All Peoples in San Francisco. He said, "One of the members-at-large of your church shares with me the materials which you send to him from time to time. It has been of the greatest inspiration to me in what I have been trying to achieve in my own community. I hope you will never let yourself become discouraged because what you are doing may seem to you to be of such little significance, as you consider the vastness of the problem that confronts us."

Often through personal correspondence with members-at-large there develops deep sharing of concerns, of success and failure, and of personal commitment. An interesting statistical note is that at the end of nine years, there were more than one thousand members-at-large in the United States and Canada, with individual members scattered throughout several countries including England, Japan, Turkey, India, and South Africa.

It was from the members-at-large that the national committee identified previously as Friends of Fellowship Church was formed. This was the committee, under the able leadership of Arthur W. Crosby, our friend the insurance executive of Philadelphia, which spearheaded the national campaign for securing the $30,000 to cover most of the cost of our first property on Larkin Street.

Included among those interested persons away from San Francisco must be the large number of students in preparatory schools, colleges, and universities whose imaginations were kindled to action as they listened to the story of this church, or looked at photographic exhibits touring their campuses which told the story more graphically than words. Most of these young people have left the college halls now and have taken their places of leadership in farflung communities. It is reasonable to hope and perhaps to assert that wherever they are, the confidence they had that religious faith can further the brotherhood of man will stay with them.

In my pastoral work with such a membership I had my most searching encounters. At the level of personal contact between minister and people the discovery is made concerning the true meaning of the common experience of fellowship. In many ways we became more and more a large family with all the hazards and strengths of that relationship.

At the close of a communion service, one of the older persons in the church challenged me because I had said in my meditation that according to the book of Mark, the last words Jesus uttered on the cross were, "My God, My God, why hast Thou forsaken me?" She found this comment extremely upsetting. "The last words Jesus said on the cross were not 'My God, My God, Why has Thou forsaken me?' but 'Father, into Thy hands do I commend my spirit.'"

"I am surprised at you," I said. "I thought you were one of my most careful listeners. What did I say exactly? Did I not say 'The last words according to the gospel of Mark, the oldest gospel'?"

Her face broke into a quizzical smile, then a full chuckle as she pointed her finger at me—"I'll catch you yet."

This kind of frank relationship expressed itself in other ways that were even harder on the ego. One Sunday when I was being accompanied by one of the officers of the church to a home where there was to be a dedication service for a baby, he asked me if I had noticed a certain visitor at church during the morning service. I said I had.

"Well, we took the same streetcar after the coffee hour. He asked me how many of the people who attended Fellowship Church understood what the minister was saying in his sermons. I told him that I thought most of us did. I, for one, understood."

Then turning to face me as we walked, he said, "But, Doc, that brings me to something I want to say to you. Don't get me wrong now. I have understood more about the meaning of religion since I have been listening to you than in all of my sixty years before I met you. Even when I don't know the words I get the meaning of what you are talking about. But, can't you use any smaller words? It would make my job easier."

I chuckled and said, "I'll certainly remember that."

"There is another thing I want to say—it is really a question I want to ask. Why do you close the Bible when you begin preaching? In all of my previous experiences in the church both before I moved from Alabama and since I have been West, the Bible is closed only at the end of the service. It announced to the Holy Spirit that you are through and He need not tarry any longer. When you close the Book it makes me just a little uneasy."

What he said brought me up with a start. My reason for closing the Book was very practical and I said, "You notice when I preach that I do not use notes or a manuscript. I lean on the Bible with my elbows very often. I discovered that this pressure tends to pull the pages apart. I close the Bible because I do not want to damage the pages. You see?"

His reply was direct and immediate: "I'll bring another big Bible for the church when you pull this one apart if you will just stop doing it."

The Image of the Church

"I'll make you a proposition," I said, "When I begin preaching and I see that you are present I'll keep the Bible open. When you are not present I'll close it."

"Fair enough."

If my congregation and I had been isolated on an island or in a valley cut off from the outside world by mountain ranges, the fact that I, a Negro, was the pastor of such a group would have made no difference so long as there was contentment in our midst. But we were not isolated. We were a part of a large metropolitan city. Daily we had to deal with the complications growing out of that fact.

For many years now, religious conferences for students or for church congregations have not been uncommon, and many of them welcome everyone regardless of race. For a white man to participate with a Negro in worship as an isolated act, but with nothing to carry over into the common life of the community, is not unheard of. For a church to establish a really successful intergroup fellowship under the leadership of a member of an ethnic minority *was* unheard of—because it was "news." To have a permanently established institution in which such things as different racial origins or cultural backgrounds were taken for granted, and to have the fellowship and the work of that institution accepted by the community was and is indeed extraordinary.

One day I had a call from a hospital to tell me that one of the members of my parish was critically ill. Before going to the hospital, I waited deliberately until the usual visiting hours because I did not on this first visit want to be in a position to have to insist on my prerogatives as a minister. When I called at the hospital to see my parishioner, I was told by the nurse in charge that Miss X was on the critical list and could see no visitors. I replied that I was not merely a visitor, I was her minister. Then the nurse did a strange thing, but I understood. She asked, "Can you spell Miss X's name?" And I said, "I will spell her name for you but it's quite unnecessary. That is not what is troubling you. Nothing in your past experience has prepared you for this—this problem. You can't understand how a responsible Caucasian member of the community could be at the same time a member of a church of which I am the minister. If she were some ne'er-do-well—that you could understand. But this particular situation is beyond you."

"Listen, you, I'm not prejudiced against Negroes!" she said a little too loudly.

I tried to reassure her: I needed first of all to remember my parishioner. "I'm not saying that you're a victim of racial prejudice Rather, you're suffering from a deep sense of being isolated, being separate, and you find it impossible to square all of this with my coming in here and saying 'I'm Miss X's minister.'"

While I was saying that, someone behind me called my name. It was another nurse who said she was Miss X's private nurse and that her patient was expecting me. Each time I visited her during the next few days, her doctor, the nurses, the interns, the orderlies on the ward, had to accommodate their thinking to this new fact in their experience. This was a famous hospital in which members of the congregation were patients many times afterward but I never had to go through that sort of thing again. The fact of Fellowship Church, what it was and what it stood for, was understood, accepted, and finally taken for granted.

Experiences with funerals were equally revealing. The first service for a member, which I held in a fashionable funeral parlor in the city, precipitated a mild crisis. The officials of this funeral home were confronted with what was to them a simply unthinkable experience. There were several conferences on the matter, in which the management expressed its main anxiety lest something happen to embarrass their long-established clientele if I held a funeral service in one of their parlors. There would not have been the same feeling had the co-minister and I officiated together. The problem arose because I was to conduct the service alone. After going through this once or twice, I was pleased to find the funeral homes accepting the fact of Fellowship Church. The attendance of an interethnic group of friends with me as minister in charge of the service was taken for granted.

Weddings? Yes, weddings too. Whenever it was relevant, in my counseling with persons who were to be married, I urged the principals to prepare their friends for the fact that I was going to perform the ceremony. This I did deliberately so that at the ceremony or after it, no one would make a thoughtless remark to one of the principals that would mar the occasion for them in any way. Despite this urging, embarrassments could not always be avoided. A young couple was being married in our residence. Because the parents of the bride were in another country at work, friends of her family came to San Francisco from a distant city to stand *in loco parentis*. They came directly to our address from the railway station. They were surprised to be greeted at the door by Mrs. Thurman who invited them into the living room and made them comfortable. Presently the bride came down, having dressed in our upstairs guest room. Then the groom entered the room and finally I came in to perform the ceremony. The tension was so dramatic that the entire ceremony was strained and difficult until the moment for the prayer. It was during the prayer that the miracle took place. At the end of the ceremony the visitors themselves talked freely with us about the shock which they had had in this first encounter with a Fellowship Church experience.

Because the question of intermarriage is the fact, or the redherring, that provides the final roadblock to realistic considerations of integration, a special comment on this whole issue must be made.

On the day that the newspapers announced that the law prohibiting the intermarriage of Caucasians and non-Caucasians was invalid, I met one fellow clergyman on the street. He said, "Well, old man, all you need is one significant interracial marriage in Fellowship Church and that'll be the end of the dream." We were very good friends. I knew his remark was facetious; yet it precipitated a very serious conversation between us about the whole matter of interracial marriage. He wanted to know something about the type of counseling that kind of marriage called for.

We were agreed that marriage, under any circumstances, requires some measure of maturity if it is to be healthy and meaningful. Marriage across racial lines adds to the need for maturity. This is true for very specific reasons:

Two such individuals should have some understanding of the social climate of American life which, as we have seen, is a climate of separateness. The opportunity for natural contacts between the races in any given community is extremely limited. The individuals, therefore, come out of two different contexts and each is afflicted with a "sense of separateness." Each context has its own etiquette, social attitudes, phobias, anxieties. Each of them has to learn more and more about the other's context.

They must be able to look upon their marriage as normal even though such an attitude may be at variance with one or the other or both of their personal contexts. In other words, either the Negro or the white community or both—and the relatives and friends involved—will probably regard the particular marriage as quite abnormal. This, for general or for specific reasons. The problem for the couple is to be mature enough to resist this social judgment. If to the principals the marriage is normal, then the chances of its survival are infinitely heightened.

They must be prepared to restrict their choices of a place to live: (a) to a certain section of the country; (b) to a certain section of the city. They may well have trouble finding suitable apartments to which they will be admitted as tenants. And be warned: each restriction tends to provoke personal conflicts which have to be resolved by understanding the prejudices and not by blaming each other.

There may be vocational restrictions. In general, the vocations in which the individual's private life is not likely to be involved present the least complications. It is so easy for a person to be penalized professionally, especially when it is the only way left by which society can penalize him, when his private life does not conform to their requirements of a "comfortable" neighbor.

It is important, particularly in this kind of marriage, to raise the question of motives which in an ingroup marriage would not be present. The reason is obvious. There may be several reasons that have little or nothing to do with the personal relationship between the two individuals. For instance: one of the parties may be trying to prove something to himself or to others. One may be attacking a family attitude or even settling a private score. One may be atoning by a kind of personal sacrifice for collective evil: "guilt expiation." One may be seeking the exotic, the bizarre, the unusual. All of these I have encountered in my own ministry. One such marriage is never a solution to any kind of intergroup social problem.

A real barrier to inclusive church membership is the possibility that such inclusiveness may lead to personal friendships and to marriage. This is true. The test of an inclusive membership is not to be found merely in the way in which people treat one another as they come together to worship Sunday morning: the test is rather in the kind and quality of the relationships among the members when they are not at church. When two people treat each other as members of the fellowship of the human race under God and continue to enjoy each other, of course there is the possibility that they may "fall in love." Understand me—I do not say it is an inevitable result—far from it. Let me repeat: I say that it is likely to happen despite the factors in the environment that operate against such a possibility. It seems to me, therefore, that a church that is committed to an inclusive membership must be prepared to accept the fact that in such a membership there will develop friendships and occasionally a marriage. To take any other position, given inclusive membership, is to be unrealistic. It is wide of the mark, however, to conclude then that an inclusive church is a breeding ground for interracial marriages. The important thing is that such a church's fellowship reveres and dignifies such marriages by providing a congenial climate of acceptance which is, never forget, a part of the Christian witness in the secular society. To see what happens when conjugal relationships across racial lines are regarded as "out of bounds" one need only look at the long agony of shame in the South from the days of slavery to now.

The church should understand what is involved in interracial marriages and be in a position to give wise counsel to any who seek the blessing of God upon their bond which may be denied the blessing of man.

One wonderful thing about Fellowship Church is the kind of words and deeds the members carry from the worship service into the community itself. The significance of this cannot be overestimated. One or two simple illustrations will suffice.

During the Christmas holidays when the church was occupying the Theatre Arts Building on Washington Street, we held several activities in the building which required special janitorial service. When I offered to pay the janitor for the extra time he said, "Of course, Doctor, I need the money. But I can't take it because for the first time in my life, I have found white people who treat me as a person. When I meet members of Fellowship Church downtown on Market Street or Grant Street, they treat me down there in the same friendly gracious way that they treat me here on Sunday morning. The least I can do to express my appreciation is to put in this extra time."

Several members of the church who had properties to rent,

either apartments or cottages, made them available to minority people because of their experience in the church. Before the "minority" family moved in, the owners did their best to help people in the immediate neighborhood to understand how they felt about fellowship. Sometimes they called on the neighbors, sometimes they invited the neighbors in. Always the position of the member was clear, but what he was trying to do was to help the people of the neighborhood to realize how little and how much it means to accept a new neighbor for what he is.

Here is another example of the church's influence on the community. At the same time that Mrs. Thurman was chairman of the Intercultural Workshop of Fellowship Church, she served in several capacities with organizations of the city that would extend the church's interest in far-flung intergroup relations. As a member of the Board of the YWCA, she was chairman of the first World Fellowship Committee, organized in the Association, bringing to bear on the local metropolitan area a very important and crucial emphasis. Before World War II, the San Francisco YWCA had well-established "Chinese" and "Japanese" branches but there had been no World Fellowship Committee, as such, composed of all units, to co-ordinate the basic concern of this organization to share essentially in the life of women and girls of all races and many faiths around the world. She served on the board of directors of the International Institute whose work was concerned primarily with the "newcomers" to our country and with a variety of programs and services that would give to them a sense of belonging in an alien environment. Because the Girls' High School was attempting at the time to weld together parents of what had become an "international" student body, Mrs. Thurman helped in the organization of its PTA and served as chairman, although we had no children of our own attending the high school. In this connection a series of afternoon teas was given in our home to which all classes in Girls' High School were invited as honored guests. One of her most significant undertakings was in developing in the local unit various aspects of the work of the National Council of Negro Women. She prepared ten articles based on extensive historical studies, in which many "old settlers" in Fellowship Church had a share. These were issued in a San Francisco newspaper and later published in book form as *Pioneers of Negro Origin in California*. This material provided an authentic resource for the active participation of the Negro community in the Centennial Celebration of the California Gold Rush, in 1949.

During the period of my ministry I served on the boards of the Council for Civic Unity, the Conference of Christians and Jews, the National Urban League, The Civil Liberties Union, the Northern California Service League, and the International Institute.

For more than two years, in a regular weekly meditation broadcast, as a public service from Fellowship Church, I developed a program called "Meditations of the Heart." On two separate occasions I was narrator with the San Francisco Symphony Orchestra in the performance of Honegger's oratorio *King David*. During one commencement, as minister of Fellowship Church, I was the Minister of the Day in the commencement exercises at the University of California, Berkeley. On almost every board of civic organizations in the city of San Francisco, including some labor unions, the membership of Fellowship Church was represented.

From what has been said, I do not mean to suggest that there has been any great social shift in the city because of the existence of Fellowship Church. These specific illustrations simply point out some of the ways by which the people of our land can at last find freedom in democracy. The existence of the church has become a beacon of truth in the minds of many, many people who in their entire lives will never enter its doors nor be involved in its active program, but who, nevertheless, came to know from our experience that the unity of fellowship is more compelling than the superstitions and credos that separate.

The celebration of the Tenth Anniversary of Fellowship Church took place at the end of my first year of absence from the active leadership of the congregation. Much of the detailed planning was carried out by a local committee under the chairmanship of Mr. George Britton and the interim minister, Dr. Dryden Phelps. Dr. Phelps had retired from a quarter of a century of active service as a missionary in China under the American Baptist Foreign Missionary Society. He brought to the period of transition a wide acquaintance with a culture fundamental in the life of the Orient.

Although I was not a part of the active ministry of Fellowship

Church during the last months of the decade, this celebration, in a sense, marked the culmination of my own ministry there.

By June, 1954, not only was Fellowship Church a vital force in the life of San Francisco and America, but also a wide variety of churches now included in their fundamental mandate a commitment to membership across lines of race and culture. Many of the historical denominations had by 1954 spelled out in detail the formal will of the people in this regard. By 1954 not only was the United Nations established and at work on many of its problems, but in that very year a scant sixty days before the celebration of our Tenth Anniversary, the historic decision of the United States Supreme Court on integration in public education was handed down. All of this is to indicate that the origin and development of Fellowship Church were part of a world-wide ferment of which many people were increasingly aware. The aim of our Tenth Anniversary celebration was to call attention to our undertaking as we paused to take a good look at the way over which we had come and to point a finger toward the future.

The celebration began on Monday, June 28, with the opening of the Children's International Workshop. The theme was "The Children of Mexico," set against the history of the workshop. A brochure stated:

Every summer for ten years, The Church for the Fellowship of All Peoples has conducted a workshop for the children of the church and community to acquaint them with people of various races and cultures. Four years ago, for instance, the study centered around the American Indian, and we had several Navajo children as guests. Three years ago, West Africa was brought to San Francisco through Nigerian students and films and art exhibits. Two years ago, India was the subject for the workshop for three exciting weeks. Last year, we chose Japan, with its interesting people and culture, its beautiful land of cherry blossoms and chrysanthemums and Fujiyama. And this year, MEXICO. . . .

Caucasian, Negro and Oriental; Protestant, Catholic, and Jew "adventure together" into the family and community life of the interesting cultures in the world.

The Church for the Fellowship of All Peoples is in its Tenth Anniversary year. What a wonderful time to address ourselves to the dream of our church which is dedicated to God, the Lord and Father of men everywhere.

The Children's Workshop for this year is Mexico. Today, Mexico, our southern neighbor, is a land of wide and growing interest. It is a land of large modern cities and Indian villages, of modernistic apartments and adobe houses.

Come along with us to Mexico. We will "adventure together" there with the children through arts and crafts, music, games and dances, stories, films, Mexican friends, and a period of quiet for gathering up all we learn. There will be a picnic, too. And remember CULMINATION DAY. Come along with us, children, to meet "Los Niños de Mexico."

During the period there were three symposia, the first one on "The Fellowship Dream" in which I gave an account of the history and development of the church, and then opened the meeting for questions and discussion.

The second symposium was "Two Aspects of the Integrated Church in Countries and Contexts Other than Ours." There were three addresses, the first, "The Church in the Orient," by Dr. Dryden Phelps. The second address, "The Church in England," was given by the Rev. Cyril Grant, who during his years as a student at the Pacific School of Religion attended Fellowship Church often, and indeed married the secretary of the church—and provided us with our first international wedding. Now he and his wife were here on a six-month leave from their church in England. The third address, "Theological Education and Preparation for Leadership in This Field," was given by Dr. Harold Ehrensperger, of the Boston University School of Theology, who graciously consented to step into the breach when Dr. Frank T. Wilson of the School of Theology at Howard University found it impossible to be present.

The third symposium was "The Integrated Church: What is Happening Today?" The first address was a discussion of certain insights from the experience of a man who had served for some time as the associate minister of The Community Church in New York City—the Rev. Maurice Dawkins, minister of The Community Church of Los Angeles. The second address, an interpretation of "The Commission Report" of the Unitarian Church on integration in the fellowship of "liberal" churches in America, was given by the Rev. Harry C. Meserve, minister of the First Unitarian Church of San Francisco. The third address, an interpretation of the experience in developing an inclusive membership in The Church of Christian Fellowship (Congregational) of Los Angeles, was given by its minister, Dr. Harold C. Kingsley.

Worship through the Fine Arts was fully accredited in the celebration by the production of *The Gospel Witch*, a verse drama written by Lyon Phelps, the son of the minister-in-residence, and produced by Olive Thurman, the daughter of the minister-at-large. The actors were of all age groups and several races. The performance was an exciting demonstration of the fact that there need be no identity between the character portrayed in a play and the particular race from which the player comes. This way of casting a play is almost unheard of on the American stage. *The Gospel Witch* has to do with the story of Ann Putnam and the Salem witch trials. It was written in the spirit rather than according to the fact of history. One line from the program is pertinent: "*The Gospel Witch* is not only a play. It is a channel, a means, a way in which a group of individuals learn about themselves in a community as large as the number in its cast, management, and audience."

The dance choir used as its theme, "Inner Horizons." This was a discourse in time, using music, the dance, and dramatic episodes as the media.

Again, notes from the program:

This liturgy was created by the members of the Liturgical Dance Group of the Church especially to celebrate the 10th Anniversary of the Church. Each member of the group under the leadership of Miss Marion Gay contributed movement, improvisation, ideas, costumes, and direction.

This worship service is provided by the members of the Liturgical Dance Group as our contribution toward the deepening religious life of the Church. We, the dancers, and you, the observers, are equally participants. Our efforts will be to evoke an atmosphere of worship in which your thoughts can wander out beyond the content we present.

Worship is an inner doing and it relates to the internal experiences and events that move by laws of their own; events that by their very nature antedate and transcend our efforts to express them verbally; events that in their present actuality affect our daily living.

It is our concern, therefore, that our dances shall lead us more and more deeply into an awareness of the meaning of this inner existence; more and more surely into acquaintance with the way life grows there, of the course it takes and the kind of doing it requires of us. Our dances become our attempt to communicate these things through the

The Image of the Church

media of movement. Communication, on the part of both dancer and observer, then rests with mutual trust and openheartedness and needs no further translation into words.

The choir sang Dett's *The Ordering of Moses*, conducted by Professor Allen C. Lannom of the School of Music of Boston University with orchestral accompaniment provided by members of the musicians' union, Local No. 6. The oratorio has to do with Moses' great commitment to the order of God to deliver the Israelites from slavery in Egypt. Rabbi Alvin Fine, a frequent pulpit guest of Fellowship Church, made available the facilities of beautiful Temple Emanu-El for this high moment of music celebration.

The committee for Adventures in Friendship presented an Oriental fashion show and potpourri of the music and arts of China, India, and Japan.

The most intimate moment during the celebration was the birthday supper held in Fellowship Hall. Here young and old, families and individuals, gathered together to share the common meal and to talk together in private reminiscence of days gone by and of dreams about the future.

The celebration closed with a dinner held in the Terrace Room of the Fairmont Hotel at which the minister-at-large and the interim minister were the principal speakers. It was appropriate that Rabbi Saul White of Temple Beth Sholoam who had preached often from our pulpit should be present with his wife as honored guests for the occasion.

At a regular board meeting of the church the treasurer introduced the fact that we were not very far-sighted if we did not consider the possibility of the sudden loss of my leadership through death. He was thinking at the moment of how we could manage in the matter of raising the budget if I were no longer present. He suggested an insurance policy on my life, made in favor of the church, and that the church, of course, would defray premium costs. I was shocked. But as the discussion developed the whole question was given a wider context. They had to prepare themselves for the possibility of a change of leadership for reasons other than death. One person put an end to the discussion by a motion to table the whole matter. This was done with manifest relief!

What happened at the board meeting, however, was reminiscent of many comments that were made to me personally as I traveled about the country talking about the church and our experience in San Francisco. For the most part there was general agreement that the church would not survive without my active leadership. Despite the fact that such comments were meant to be complimentary, I regarded them as a reflection upon my own leadership as well as an expression of unfaith.

It is true that in a sense I "called" the membership, whereas usually the membership calls its minister. Many of our members, at first, believed with my belief until they were able to believe with their own belief. I was constantly harassed by the reference to Thurman followers while, with all of my heart, I wanted them to have a sense of God rather than a sense of Thurman. Perhaps no sentiment occurred more in my own private prayer life than that my ego would not come between the people and God. The uniqueness of our kind of religious fellowship made this extremely difficult, except in the primary acts of worship themselves. There never was a question in my mind as to the rightness and soundness of our undertaking. It seemed incredible to me that our survival as a religious fellowship could possibly be dependent upon any human individual. To me, always, Fellowship Church was the work of God. Many there were who would say always, "You'll see what will happen."

5. A Radical Test

IN THE WINTER OF 1953, I was invited to become Dean of Marsh Chapel and Professor of Spiritual Disciplines and Resources at Boston University. Here was an opportunity to see whether there could be established in a large urban university a center of worship in which the experience of Fellowship Church could be shared in the restricted environment of an academic community. Unlike Howard University, this was predominantly an institution of more than twenty thousand students, in which the great majority of the personnel were Caucasian. Also to make such a move away from the church would provide a radical test that would determine significantly the survival value of the unique ideas upon which the church was founded. It was a most difficult decision to make because my life was profoundly committed to, and involved in, the life of the church and there was a sense of weariness even in contemplating another pioneering adventure. The emotional strain to myself—and to my family as well—to move into a situation in which we would seem to be living in a "fish bowl" as a Negro carrying such grave responsibility in a white institution could only be absorbed by an authentic sense of spiritual necessity. After many days of meditation, searching of motives, and prayer, the decision was made.

The following spring I was granted an indefinite leave of absence effective September 1, 1953. I was given the title "Minister-at-Large" which made it possible for me to continue as an active worker for the church whenever I was needed and to maintain a relationship between me and the congregation which I needed, but one that would not involve me in the day-to-day problems and decisions. This would give the minister of the church and his official family complete responsibility for the guidance of the church, without formal or informal reference to ideas that I might have. There was an understanding between the church and the administration of Boston University that I would be at liberty to preach at the church in the summer if that fitted the wishes of the church and my own plans. It was further agreed that I would represent the church whenever I could by keeping alive the active interest of members-at-large and by continuing to make friends for the idea. One tangible expression of my continuing interest has been my writing of an annual Christmas card for the church, and the holding of religious retreats for the congregation each summer.

The question of the survival of the church without my active leadership is now no longer theoretical. What happened in the interim period between my leaving and the calling of a full-time permanent minister and the life of the church under the leadership of the permanent minister?

When I decided to come to Boston University, the board—and I as a member of it—took great care to prepare the congregation for my withdrawal. At many board meetings we discussed every ramification of the problem we could think of as we planned for the future. The board appointed a Committee of Twenty-five for a self-study of the congregation, and of the program, the religious leadership, and finances. Meanwhile there was a special committee made up largely of members of the board who were to work with the interim minister, Dr. Phelps, in scheduling the preachers for the Sunday services. During the period of his leadership the form of the program grew as it had under my leadership. Lynn Buchanan, the program director during my ministry, remained for a year after I left.

My leaving discouraged some and some despaired. There was a temporary slackening of interest and a marked falling away in attendance: a few members withdrew from the church. This was to be expected, but fortunately the members of the congregation began to realize that the responsibility for the life of the church rested squarely on their shoulders and not on the shoulders of any single man. When I returned that first summer, I found that the people who were members and others in the congregation were participating in the affairs of the church, as individuals, with a growing sense of personal responsibility.

The second period began with the interim pastor, but later the church extended an invitation to the Rev. Francis Geddes, to become its full-time minister with the informal understanding that there would be a preliminary period of working together during which the church and the minister would have an opportunity to discover what the will of God was for them. The church was very fortunate when it called Mr. Geddes. He had worked at the church as a summer intern during the last years of his undergraduate life at Stanford University and had served as a summer assistant during a part of his theological training at Yale University. At the end of his course at Yale, he was invited to become full-time assistant minister of the church. This term of service coincided with my last year as minister-in-residence. Unfortunately he was unable to complete the full year because of illness. Upon his recovery he became a Congregational minister in a neighboring county and it was from this ministry that he was called to Fellowship Church. He is, therefore, a person whose early professional church experience is deeply rooted in Fellowship Church. He was ordained in the Congregational Church but in a real sense he is a spiritual son of The Church for the Fellowship of All Peoples. The significance of this cannot be overestimated; he was already oriented before he assumed the leadership. The leadership had shifted from a Negro minister to a white minister. Nevertheless, through all the shifts in leadership, the same emphasis on the commitment of the life to God has continually expressed itself in the kind of inclusive programming which characterizes the church. Our church's life is centered in worship, in the strength our worship of God gives us. It recognizes that our good will is nurtured by our knowledge and understanding of people and peoples. It recognizes our need to keep on striving to understand and cherish our religious experiences. It knows that the religious education of children is important, and it has learned better ways to train them. It knows how important it is to help a community to know our church's reason for being and its commitment.

Under the leadership of Mr. Geddes, the church now participates more than ever in the organized religious life of the city of San Francisco. In the past the church was a member of the Council of Churches, although not taking part in all of its activities. Now the congregation participates—actively—in the Council's deliberations.

A recent boon to the church in the form of a ranch has added immeasurably to the quality and degree of fellowship within the congregation. The name of the ranch is "Stonetree," located in the beautiful Valley of the Moon about an hour's drive north of San Francisco. For many years it was the home of Mr. and Mrs. Edward A. Small and their family. It was Mr. Small's vision that led him to build a simple but well-appointed large house as the family residence and to surround it with several small cottages on the edge of a thriving grove of redwood trees. Here through the years friends of the parents and friends of the children were invited. The beauty of the surroundings and the wide variety of persons who came and went enriched the family with a deeper understanding of the meaning of life and the significance of *human* relations.

When Mr. Small died in the spring of 1955, the children had grown and were no longer living at home. Slowly Mrs. Small adjusted herself to the idea that she could not carry on there alone. To part with the place was unthinkable. The idea of making it available to some suitable group as a memorial to Mr. Small, whose vision created it, appealed to the whole family.

While one of the sons, Bill, was in the East he was a guest of our home in Boston. We talked about the ranch and the desire of the family for its use. The place seemed to be made for Fellowship Church. Mr. Geddes, our minister, had been for two years prior to his return to Fellowship Church, the minister of the local church to which the Smalls belonged. He was intimately acquainted with the family and had been a guest at the ranch many times. As pastor and friend he stood beside the family through the terminal illness of Mr. Small and the difficult days of adjustment that followed.

This is the picture that Mrs. Small herself gives of what is happening:

> The unplanned combinations of people who sometimes share Stonetree for a weekend of rest and recreation coalesce into a congenial group. As often as possible church groups come here for meetings of planning committees and conferences. People seem more creative in their thinking when city restrictions are removed, and ideas can be more freely expressed. Of special value is the opportunity for members to become better acquainted on an informal basis, and to form new friendships. . . .
>
> Although those of us who have been associated with Fellowship

A Radical Test

Church have come to regard the interracial feature as natural, visitors are sometimes surprised at this smooth-running, integrated group. One Sunday last summer two students from Iran, who were attending Eastern colleges, visited Fellowship Church in San Francisco. They were invited to a work party at the ranch the following Saturday. When they arrived they were equipped with overalls and put to work on some clearing projects. At noon they joined the group for lunch in the patio where some of the church women provided a hearty meal for the hungry workers. There was a spirit of "camaraderie" and obvious enjoyment and an easy feeling of good fellowship. The foreign students kept expressing their amazement. One of them said, "I did not believe such a thing would be possible here. It contradicts the many stories I have heard of racial prejudice in the United States."

... I have been impressed by the effect the place has on strangers who know nothing of our family or our life at Stonetree. The things we sought and found were so simple and yet so apparently hard to implement in the modern tempo. One key to it, I think, and the reason so much of my husband's personality is communicated to others, is that he planned and worked in close harmony with nature, and with love for what he was doing. The genuineness and beauty of his spirit are sensed through the home he created, and call out a true and genuine response in others. Thus at Stonetree, Fellowship Church finds it easy to carry out its ideals and to demonstrate that in spite of all the divisive and hostile forces in our world picture, people of different races can associate harmoniously if they have the will to do so.[1]

Perhaps the most distinguishing characteristic of Fellowship Church is the fact that the intergroup fellowship which is experienced in the worship of God on Sunday is but one more dimension of sharing which many of the members enjoy as well in various phases of their community life. The resident members of the church are scattered from Palo Alto to Martinez, yet the sense of community has developed in spite of distance. The remarkable aptitude of the church is that its members strive together toward common goals or meet for simple pleasures even when they are not at the church: having coffee together in a favorite restaurant or in a member's home; having dinner together at home or in a restaurant; planning a theater party, say, for fourteen; meeting downtown to shop; going together to visit the sick; being available to baby-sit; sharing grief over the death of a friend. This

[1] From the *Vassar Alumnae Magazine*, February, 1958, pp. 6–7.

is a community, a community reaching far beyond a neighborhood.

The conveniences of the ranch and its delightful surroundings have opened more and more opportunities for the experience of community. Families enjoy weekends together. A dozen women might spend Friday afternoon and Saturday picking and canning blackberries for church affairs or to sell them to help the treasury. Groups up to thirty go to the ranch for an overnight retreat. Church committees hold meetings there in the beauty and quiet to think and feel their way into plans for the future. "Stonetree" has made it far easier for a member to move into the center of the life of the church than ever before.

Whatever the future, one important fact remains—that the existence of The Church for the Fellowship of All Peoples in the city of San Francisco for fourteen years provides an exciting "for instance" of what a single institution under God can do to lift the ceiling of hope for all men of good will, the hope that a common fellowship inspired by the worship of God is the forerunner of His Kingdom on earth. The vision of Kyber Pass found fulfillment in our experience of and with Fellowship Church. This experience has not provided a final nor a complete answer to the question of the exclusiveness of the church both as to conditions of belonging and as to race. But it gives me confidence about the direction in which to continue the search. The theological basis of membership in the Christian church at large continues to provide grounds for active discrimination between the saved and the unsaved—however this whole matter may be rationalized by the Christian liberal. The racial basis of membership continues to provide grounds for active discrimination between Negro and white. Over against both of these I put the fact of the continuing existence of Fellowship Church as a religious fellowship in which the basic spiritual requirement is the integrity of the quest for, and the centrality of the commitment to, God. And in addition to this fact there is the movement of the Holy Spirit of God manifesting Himself throughout the church on behalf of "experienced community" in new ways that give fresh hope to all who strive for the realization of the Kingdom of God on the earth.

Conclusion

I AM CONVINCED that it is possible to develop a religious fellowship which is so unifying in its quality that the barriers originally separating its members one from another will gradually disappear, leaving in their stead a new sense of community. While it was necessary in 1944 to develop our fellowship outside of the context of regular denominations, the same would not be true today, for the reason that Protestant Christianity is today more congenial to the experience of brotherhood within the church than was true a decade ago. This does not mean that the practice of brotherhood within the church is general, but for the first time in its history, the church in America is on the defensive. This defensive attitude quite paradoxically tends to create a climate in which it may become more and more reasonable for people to have experiences of unity in religious fellowship that are more compelling than the concepts, the prejudices, and the fears that divide.

As difficult as it is for experiences of unity to transcend differences of race, it is infinitely more difficult to create experiences of unity that can unite beyond the fundamental creeds that divide. There is an amazing incongruity in the fact that in peripheral matters there is fellowship, there is community, but in the central act of celebration of the human spirit in the worship of God, the lines are tightly drawn and a man goes before God with those only who believe as he does. The experience that should unite all men as children of one Father becomes the great divider that separates a man from his brothers.

Epilogue

... *What is the climate in 1959?*

The armed services by formal intent are no longer segregated. The District of Columbia has an integrated public school system, most of its hotels are open to Negroes, and practically all public facilities such as restaurants and theaters no longer honor the color bar. In many sections of the South, the facilities of public parks are open to all citizens. The nonsegregation of interstate passengers by train, bus, and plane is becoming increasingly normal. In certain cities such as Montgomery, Alabama, the issue of segregation on public buses is being resolved. The 1954 Supreme Court Decision concerning segregation of schools made of national significance a public issue beyond the practice merely of the maintenance of educational provision; further, the whole matter of the right to vote is being scrutinized with the view of the eradication of discriminatory practices. In fine, segregation as a part of the American way of life is being increasingly challenged on all fronts which have to do with the common life.

What about the church? As a result of the Supreme Court's decision on the desegregation of public schools, most of the national religious bodies in their formal conclaves have made pronouncements reflecting their interpretation of the significance of this decision in terms of the practices and the policy of their local churches:[1]

THE AMERICAN BAPTIST CONVENTION: We commend the U.S. Supreme Court in its historic decision of 1954 outlawing segregation in public education. . . . We fully support the Supreme Court's decision and deplore the resistance to this decision in certain states where integration of public education has met organized opposition.

---

[1] Tuskegee Institute Studies on Desegregation in the Church.

Epilogue

SOUTHERN BAPTIST CONVENTION: We recognize the fact that this Supreme Court decision is in harmony with the constitutional guarantee of equal freedom to all citizens, and with the Christian principles of equal justice and love for all men. We urge our people and all Christians to conduct themselves in this period of adjustment in the spirit of Christ; we pray that God may guide us in our thinking and our attitudes to the end that we may help and not hinder the progress of justice and brotherly love; . . .

CHURCH OF THE BRETHREN: We note with appreciation all recent steps made in the direction of elimination of segregation, including the decision of the Supreme Court interpreting the Constitution as opposing segregation in the public schools. We appeal to our Brethren to lead out in effecting these social changes in every area of life. . . .

CONGREGATIONAL CHRISTIAN CHURCHES: We call upon all Americans to undertake timely and tolerant implementation of the Supreme Court's decision, and that our Department of Race Relations and the Council for Social Action carry forward such activities as will develop public support for the Supreme Court decision.

INTERNATIONAL CONVENTION OF DISCIPLES OF CHRIST: We approve and commend the decision of the Supreme Court concerning segregation in the public schools. . . .

PROTESTANT EPISCOPAL: The 58th General Convention of the Protestant Episcopal Church in the U.S.A. now commends to all the clergy and people of this church that they accept and support this ruling of the Supreme Court, and that by opening channels of Christian conference and communication between the races concerned in each diocese and community, they anticipate constructively the local implementation of this ruling as the law of the land.

EVANGELICAL AND REFORMED CHURCH: We must say plainly that to attempt to evade integration in the public schools by actions which would weaken or undermine the public schools is wrong. . . .

EVANGELICAL UNITED BRETHREN CHURCH: We express our gratitude for the unanimous decision of the U.S. Supreme Court that segregation "in the public schools is unconstitutional." We urge our church members to assist in preparing their communities psychologically and spiritually for implementing the . . . decision. . . . We call upon our local churches, annual conferences, colleges and theological seminaries, boards and institutions to implement this decision so that men everywhere may be lifted to new levels of social responsibility and new dimensions of human brotherhood.

AMERICAN LUTHERAN CHURCH: We fully support the

Supreme Court decision and deplore the resistance to this decision in certain states. . . .

AUGUSTANA EVANGELICAL LUTHERAN: We urge our members to use their influence in the securing of full rights of citizenship for all. . . .

UNITED LUTHERAN CHURCH IN AMERICA: The ULCA, recognizing its deep involvement in the moral crisis confronting the U.S.A. in the current controversy over desegregation occasioned by the Supreme Court decision of May 17, 1954, affirms the statement on Human Relations adopted by the Executive Board of the ULCA and the Board of Social Missions (April 1951), and calls upon all its congregations and people, exercising Christian patience and understanding, to work for the fullest realization of the objectives of that statement. . . . Our congregations are encouraged to contribute to the solution of the problem by demonstrating in their own corporate lives the possibility of integration. . . .

AFRICAN METHODIST EPISCOPAL CONNECTIONAL COUNCIL: We commend the Supreme Court for this far-reaching decision, and urge the support and cooperation of our entire constituency in its implementation.

AFRICAN METHODIST EPISCOPAL ZION: Thanking God for the Supreme Court decision . . . recommending to our far-flung constituency . . . active cooperation with local school boards in implementing the program of immediate desegregation. . . .

CHRISTIAN METHODIST EPISCOPAL CHURCH: We commend the Supreme Court of the U.S. for its heroic and just decision regarding the matter of declaring segregated schools to be unconstitutional; . . .

METHODIST GENERAL CONFERENCE: The decisions of the Supreme Court of the U.S. relative to segregation made necessary far-reaching and often difficult community readjustments throughout the nation. We call upon our people to effect these adjustments in all good faith, with brotherliness and patience. . . .

PRESBYTERIAN CHURCH IN THE U.S.: General Assembly, 1954: The Assembly commends the principle of the decision and urges all members of our churches to consider thoughtfully and prayerfully the complete solution of the problem involved. . . .

PRESBYTERIAN CHURCH IN THE U.S.: General Assembly, 1957: The General Assembly would call attention to the fact that the Christian faith has never countenanced racial discrimination and that the Supreme law of the land requires that it no longer be practiced in the public school system. . . .

PRESBYTERIAN CHURCH IN THE U.S.A.: General Assembly,

1954: We receive with humility and thanksgiving the recent decision of our Supreme Court. . . .
UNITED PRESBYTERIAN CHURCH OF NORTH AMERICA: We believe the United Presbyterian Church has always believed in the integration of the races . . . we thank God that the laws of the land have made segregation illegal in education.
THE ROMAN CATHOLIC CHURCH: Pope Pius XI denounced the "so-called myth of race and blood," and his successor, Pope Pius XII, said that "there remains no other way to salvation than that of repudiating definitely the pride of race and blood and to turn resolutely to the spirit of sincere brotherhood which is founded on the worship of the Divine Father of all."

This is an important sampling of the formal positions of some of the major historic Christian denominations in the United States concerning the issue of racial segregation. The state has spoken through a series of decisions by the Supreme Court of the land. The national church bodies have spoken. In the light of these pronouncements from the church and the state, what is happening at the level of the local church in the local community, U.S.A.? It is important to say that at the present moment there is a ferment at work on the side of inclusiveness in church membership. In almost every community in the North, East, and West, and in many parts of the South, there are local churches that are grappling with the grim realities of this problem with the firm intent to change old habit patterns of race segregation within their fellowships. The fact remains, however, that in the year 1959, by and large, the church continues to be a segregated institution.

But let us take a closer look. This situation is due to several factors. There is first and foremost the deeply ingrained social behavior pattern. The United States of America is in fact dedicated to the separation of the races. Wherever it does not appear, it is the exception rather than the rule. The will of the American people continues to resist all movements that would undermine the validity of segregation as indigenous to the American way of life. The Christian church reflects this fact, despite official pronouncements both of church and state. The resistance does not seem to be influenced by loyalty to Christ or devotion to His Kingdom on the earth. It ignores the handwriting on the wall that the planet is a small neighborhood owing to the annihilation of space and time. It is unable to deal with the fact that the earth's population is predominantly non-Caucasian and that any national feeling of separation on the basis of race and color jeopardizes the future of the human race and destroys the possibility of peace for the generations yet to be.

Nothing less than a major revolution in the human spirit can hope to alter this crystallized pattern of behavior. Confronted with this stubborn fact, how may the local church share in bringing about a change? This is the crucial question. Let it be clearly understood that neither the minister nor the church knows precisely how to accomplish the change. The life of Fellowship Church is but one honest attempt to find a way. The suggestions that follow come out of a life-long wrestling with this sickness in the soul of America.

The minister is a man. He is the child of his culture. He reflects in his life the forces and the ideas that have cradled him and by which he has been nurtured. By vocation and personal commitment he is Christian. This means that the gospel of Christ which he proclaims as a professional is also the basis upon which he lives privately before God. His is the unique vocation in the sense that what he is dedicated to be as a Christian minister is identical with what is his dedication as a Christian man.

As he faces the issue of the implementation of the mandate of the secular state and that of his particular denomination concerning the practice of brotherhood as between Negro and white in the common life, he may honestly decide that such mandates are in error. It is possible for him to be of the mind that God is either white or that it is His will that the white man dominate the earth to His glory—that the significance of the nonwhite peoples, particularly those of African descent, can be determined only by the degree to which they become means for the fulfillment of the lives of white men. If this is the destiny of the white portion of humanity and it is for this that they were created, such a position is beyond all argument and all facts. I have encountered such men in my time. In talking with them I had the sense of being in the presence of some form of life that was not human. Here was not meanness nor mere prejudice, no hatred was manifest—only deadness and stark moral desolation. However, it is such ministers who can very easily become the rallying point for organized hate and for movements that frustrate and undermine the intent of the state and the church in the matter of brotherhood at the level of the local community.

Or again the minister may be a kindly man who in his most personal relations practices the gospel of love in matters involving people of other groups, including Negroes. In his community, North or South, his love is manifest and dependable. It is a part of his practicing faith to befriend, to succor, and to bless. And yet he may be convinced that the church is the heavenly community set down in the world—it is a place of refuge for those who would escape from the world into salvation. His view is that the world is evil, utterly and completely evil, and is only waiting its final destruction as the Judgment of God against sin and corruption. The question of membership integration is never raised as such. If a man believes and will yield his life, that is all that matters. Attitudes on race are completely beside the point. It is for this reason that such religious fellowships as the Jehovah's Witnesses, and certain holiness sects even in the deep South, are often inclusive in their membership. The conditions for membership do not include ethnic, cultural, or national considerations. Inclusiveness is incidental, never crucial. If such is the position, then it follows almost automatically that racial prejudice as a general attitude will be undermined, or better, uprooted. By inference from the kind of religious experience evident in the life of the group, racial prejudice becomes a road block to salvation. In order to welcome anyone who believes and yields his life to God, without regard to color, sex, or origin, the group, in the very nature of the case, must be without prejudices to color, sex or origin. What is indicated here is that it is quite possible for a religious fellowship to function with its leader in even a Southern community, ignoring the behavior pattern of racial segregation. This is the fact. To be sure, such a group is queer, is "out of bounds," is regarded as being on the fringes of respectability. But here it is a living witness to fact. Such groups were functioning long before 1954 or before there was any general awakening of the conscience of the American people in the Christian church.

This fact suggests that the whole picture would have been very different in American life if there had been included in Christian orthodoxy a judgment which said that racial prejudice would debar a man from salvation. Here I have no immediate reference to the fringe demands of salvation—but to the central demand. Suppose there had been the insistence that to be born again, to accept Jesus Christ as Savior and Lord, a man must be free of prejudices based upon color or "race." Such prejudice would be defined, therefore, as mortal sin and the harboring of it would jeopardize a man's eternal soul. Racial prejudice, then, would create in such a person the kind of guilt that would separate him from God and his Christ. If this had been a part of Christian orthodoxy, then the enormous energy and vitality which evidence themselves wherever orthodoxy prevails would have been reflected in an experienced democracy in American life. This would have accomplished what no mere social gospel or liberal Christianity could effect. The purification of the life, the redemption of the spirit, the salvation of the soul, would not be possible for a man who closed his door against his fellows, whatever may be their status, color, or position in the world. Such a position would define for the believer the things for which he must stand with his life and the things against which he must stand. Social responsibility would be the inevitable result flowing from his experience of personal redemption.

Let us assume that the local church and its minister, or either one of them, accept the pronouncement of their national body in solemn assembly. What then? What does such a local church do when the issues burst forth in his Southern community? Many indeed are the articles written and studies made in an attempt to discover and report on this question. There is scarcely a religious periodical of national circulation that has not devoted many pages to a discussion of the wide variety of reactions to the demands of the explosive social situation.

Where could such a minister begin? He may recognize initially that the spirit that had resulted in a unanimous ruling against segregation was inspired by the same spirit which had tutored men in the awareness that God is the Father of mankind and all are His children. This is an anthropomorphic statement but what it expresses essentially is the oneness of life. Therefore for the minister, it is not necessary for him to justify his attitude by any political response whatsoever. He can rest his case on the gospel of the Kingdom of God and the great commandment where Judaism and Christianity meet in creative synthesis. He can consider this binding upon himself, his family, and his congregation.

Even so, he may not become involved in the wider community struggle.

Or the minister may seek deliberately to involve himself in the community and its struggle. But until the issue was forced by a court decision he was prohibited by the fact that unbrotherliness in practice had the sanction of law and order. Segregation and all that went with it was a part of the respectable and respected way of life sanctioned by custom and guaranteed by law. Once the legal sanction was removed the minister was forced to face the issue and to take a stand either for segregation and against the ruling of the Highest Court of the land or against segregation and for the ruling of the Highest Court of the land. There is no time now for platitudes and the pious phrase—the minister must make a fateful decision. For the first time in his life he may raise the question as to the teaching of his own religious faith concerning such matters. He is the leader of his congregation, their counselor, and their shepherd! What does he do?

In quick order he has to dismiss several alternatives—the church must be the church and not be contaminated by involvement in social struggles—he may withdraw from all local committees or organizations which by structure will be drawn into the struggle —he may accept a post in the North, one which has been dangling before him for some time—he may be forced to resign and thereby become unemployable, perhaps.

But suppose he stays functioning as the good shepherd? As is his custom and his discipline, he turns to God—he makes the crisis a matter of prayer and much searching in the Presence of God. Here he may discover how deep is the gulf that separates him truly from his Negro neighbor and brother. Probably such a consideration had never previously become a matter of prayer and meditation. In his sustained wrestling with the issue before God he makes the terrifying discovery that the Negro has never been regarded by him as an equal, however defined. He reviews his life to discover that even though he has grown up with Negroes in his Southern community, he has associated with them as a white man. He has never tried to identify with them, to sit where they sit, to feel as they feel, to look out upon life through their troubled eyes. With God's help this he must now do and willingly. At last in his struggle he is able to say to God, "Search me, O God, and know my heart: try me, and know my thoughts: and see if there be any wicked way in me, and lead me in the way everlasting." He emerges from his spiritual crisis deeply chastened and a new sense of community without boundaries begins to make revolutionary demands upon his total life pattern. Not only must there be some statement as catharsis for his guilt but included in his Christian commitment is a privately relayed sense of social responsibility.

First of all the minister recognizes that a change of heart is not enough. Zeal that does not have a hard core of sustaining fact is likely to destroy what it would save and protect. Such a minister begins to gather data. He reads the decision of the Court. From a legal friend he is able to get the long series of former decisions leading up to this fateful one. He discovers that it has never occurred to him to question how Jim Crow, segregation, got started. There must be a history of this thing—or did it spring full grown as Athena from the head of Zeus? Upon inquiry he discovers a book such as C. V. Woodward's *The Strange Career of Jim Crow*. Again he rereads the pronouncements from his own denomination concerning these matters. He turns to the Book and examines anew the life and the teachings of the Master. He shares his thoughts and his findings with those of his fellow ministers who, by experience, are congenial in spirit and ideas. He may find hope or discouragement here. In all of this the companion of his life, his wife, may have moved step by step with him.

The effect of all of this scrutiny begins to appear first in his public or pastoral prayers and then as overtones in his sermons. Up to this point he has not counseled his congregation from the pulpit. He is wrestling with a real ambivalence about doing so. Should he preach a sermon or a series of sermons on this question showing what is demanded of those who claim to be followers of Christ? Or should he call a special meeting of his congregation for the purpose of discussing out in the open the whole issue that the community faces and to see if as a church there is a willingness to take a stand—or to discover how his own situation would be threatened when his position is clearly known? Which?

But before the question is resolved he is told that his leading layman is taking the initiative in organizing a unit of the White Citizens Council. He goes to see him. He is shocked by the fact that his layman was sure that the minister could be counted on to support the organization. There is searching talk between them.

Epilogue

Here in this layman is a gentle kind of man who could always be counted upon to do the gracious and the Christian thing—but in this matter he is adamant. The minister discovers with his friend what the country as a whole has slowly discovered—that racial prejudice has stained the mind and the conscience of America and that like a dreaded sickness it has poisoned the will and paralyzed the intent to community. It becomes understandable, however lamentably so, how a governor can dare to close the public schools and turn to the churches for classroom accommodations while the parents of some of the children look on with despair and with futility. This is the sickness of the soul which the minister recognizes now in his leading layman. He tries to understand him. He tells him the journey over which he, his minister, has come up to the present time. They pray together. The minister looks deep into his eyes as he says, "This is wrong, John. The whole monstrous thing is evil and I must oppose it with everything I have. I am no martyr but as a follower of Christ I have no choice. May God have mercy on all of us."

His course of action is now clear to him. He tells his official board where he stands and as best he can, makes his position understood in the light of the meaning of Christian religious experience. He expresses a hope that they will support him but if they do not, this fact will not alter the necessity under which he must labor and function. As the leader of his congregation, he must next interpret to his congregation what the gospel has to say in this important issue. He is deeply beloved by his congregation. He finds that there are people in his congregation who think as he does and who had wondered why he had been so long taking a stand around which they themselves could rally. But there are others who withdrew in anger as those who have been betrayed in the house of a friend. Before his God, before his people, and before the community he stands giving his witness to the binding character of his Christian ethic. From this point he seeks deliberately to do those things that will implement the intent to community as expressed by the Court, by the Church, and by his Lord. No one can give a blueprint as to what is the best procedure. Many experiments must be made, all of the resources of the community must be tapped. A wise suggestion from Mahatma Gandhi to Muriel Lester many years ago speaks to the point. "See everyone who in any way can contribute to the cause. Do not be discouraged by those who turn you away. You must make their rejection your strength."

In January, 1959, after the final revision of this manuscript, I gave the sermon at the Brotherhood meeting of the Houston Council on Race Relations in Education. At this meeting Pastor Paul Seastrand was awarded a plaque by the Council for his leadership in guiding his congregation, the Augustana Lutheran Church, through the experiences leading to the integration of his church.

The story of the Augustana Lutheran Church, Houston, Texas, illustrates what may be done when a Southern church meets the challenge of a changing neighborhood.[1] Pastor Seastrand was called to become the minister of that church in 1948. At that time the edge of the Negro residential area was some five blocks away. In 1952 the Negro population began to move toward the vicinity of the church. The congregation became increasingly ill at ease in the presence of this encroachment. A public expression of the minister's convictions seemed mandatory.

The first public statement bearing on the issue was made at the annual meeting of the congregation in January, 1954. In his pastoral report, Pastor Seastrand wrote:

> The infiltration of Negroes in our community is seemingly a cause for some concern, and we find ourselves inescapably confronted with a situation which challenges our Christian faith and behavior. Are we going to ignore them altogether or are we going to respect them as souls for whom Christ died and for whom the Gospel is intended just as much as for ourselves. Whatever we do, let Augustana conduct herself in a way that is positively Christian, and seeking the motivation of the Holy Spirit, let us resolve to approach this problem as we honestly believe the Lord Jesus Himself would do it. To act in any way that is contrary to the Spirit of Christ is to accentuate the problem and to harm ourselves.

There were two persons who registered their opposition to the statement. The purpose of the statement was to take full cognizance of the challenge facing the congregation and to acquaint them with the pastor's position as well as his interpretation of the Christian position. At this time no effort was made at direct contact with any Negroes in the neighborhood.

[1] A pamphlet telling this story is available from the church.

Up to the annual meeting in 1954, the minister had not preached on the theme. But on Sunday, July 4, 1954, Pastor Seastrand preached a sermon on "The Responsibility of Augustana to the Community." The sermon was given a good hearing. A few expressed agreement, many respected the minister's conviction. There was only one instance of record which indicated marked bitterness.

While the minister was away on vacation during most of the month of July, at his request the vice-chairman of the Board of Deacons called a meeting to discuss the issues quite thoughtfully. Pastor Seastrand's idea was to make full fresh discussion easier in his absence. He wanted to know what the formal position of the board was in this crucial matter. After much thoughtful discussion the following resolution was passed:

> We the members of the Board of Deacons, as a testimony and witness of our faith in our Lord Jesus Christ have caused to be composed and recorded in the minutes of meetings of the Church Council the following resolution: Be it resolved that we do here and now reaffirm our support of Pastor Seastrand in his every endeavor to further God's influence in the community, seeking out souls regardless of color or nationality. We are ready to examine and pass on applications for membership in the congregation of all persons without regard for color or nationality.

The vote was 6 to 2 with one absentee.

In September, 1954, a parish worker was employed to make a formal survey of the neighborhood. No invitations were extended to Negroes at that time. The primary purpose of the survey was to make formal contact with the people in the immediate area of the church.

There was an atmosphere of marked tension and anxiety in the congregation but it is interesting to point out that according to a statement of the minister, only one person, among those who were in opposition, came to talk the matter over. He stated further that his greatest opposition came from Northerners and not from Southerners. Some of his warmest supporters were among those persons born and raised in the South.

At the annual meeting on January 11, 1955, the minister gave a lengthy section of his report to more guided discussion of the issue. To his surprise all other matters were discussed and a motion for adjournment was made without any reference to the issue that was in everybody's mind.

After this meeting the parish worker was requested to extend the invitation to any persons in the community to worship in the church. But it was not until Sunday, March 27, that the first Negroes came. The minister was surprised to see these two Negro women even though he had hoped that there would be some response to the general community invitation. There was a crescendo of murmuring in the congregation but no incident.

At the next meeting of the Board of Administration, the pastor was asked directly if Negroes were being invited to the church: He replied: "As pastor of this Christian congregation and as one who is primarily accountable to the Lord Jesus Christ, ALL people in this community are being issued the invitation to worship in our church."

There were some who felt that if Negroes came the church would have to tolerate them, but they should not be invited.

At a regular board meeting in May a motion was made to appoint a committee to study ways and means for relocating the church. After much discussion the motion was defeated by a two-thirds majority. There were attempts made to call a special meeting of the congregation to decide about admitting Negroes to membership. This move the minister, with the body of the leaders of the church, resisted.

The dam broke in June, 1955, when the summer Vacation Bible School became interracial for the first time. On opening day there were no Negro children. Things changed radically when the minister saw several children in different yards looking over towards the church on opening day. He waved to them; they waved back. The next morning they came.

Gradually the church became identified as one whose doors of Christian fellowship were open to all. Even so there was no mass movement of the Negroes in the neighborhood to the church. Despite this fact there were some members of the church who could not remain even with a single Negro in the membership. By the end of 1955, eighteen confirmed members severed their relationship with the church—but during the same period twenty-six adults became affiliated. At this time there were six Negro children enrolled in the church school.

Epilogue

At the annual meeting in January, 1956, the minister in his message quoted the following sentences from Dr. Conrad Hoyer, Executive Secretary of the Division of American Missions of the National Lutheran Council:

> Lutheran Churches, as churches of Jesus Christ, are His creation and not our own, and inclusiveness is of the very nature of the Church. No local church has any more right to decide to be racially or culturally exclusive than it has to modify or abandon any article of faith.

It was decided at this meeting that the time had come to invite Negroes into the full fellowship of the congregation as members. This meant that they would be invited to enroll in the Pastor's Inquiry Class, make application for membership, be accepted by the Board of Deacons, and be received through confirmation at a Sunday morning worship service before the congregation. A Negro family consisting of mother, father, and two children ages thirteen and fifteen, joined the class and on Sunday morning, May 7, 1956, together with nine white persons became members of the church.

What about the minister and the church in the North? And in this category I put the Negro church, North or South.

First, what about the white church that is in a neighborhood that is changing from Caucasian to Negro or to some other so-called ethnic minority? The obvious way out of the situation is to follow its white members into the district to which they have moved. This means to vacate the property and, usually, to sell it to the newcomers. This has been the pattern in many cities in the United States. It is only in recent years that the kind of conscience has developed within the Christian community which condemns this action as an excuse not to face the problem of the changing neighborhood.

An alternative to moving is to develop a program that meets community needs for recreation and various kinds of community service for any and all while the formal religious Sunday services are maintained strictly as the one unbroken link between the church and its "white" members. Under such circumstances a few of the newcomers may occasionally drift into the Sunday service, but this is not likely. Notice how morality submits to prejudice. A church recognizes that it has a responsibility to those who live in its district and it seeks to meet that responsibility of community service; but, if you please, there is no reason to recognize those people as regular participating members of the congregation. This, true, is caste discrimination as much as it is ethnic discrimination. Even so, it is somewhat better than to vacate the neighborhood entirely.

A second alternative to moving the church is to try to make the people who are coming into the neighborhood feel not only welcome but comfortable in what for them is a new experience in a new environment. Good will isn't enough; it takes more than good will. Does it really help to post on a bulletin board the notice that all people are welcome? Does it help to pay for an extra line in the weekly newspaper saying that the church has an open door to all who come? Or rather, do such announcements tend to raise barriers because they have in them the kind of patronage which so outrages self-respect?

Many feel—and I am one—that the church must make a formal decision to stay where it is located. This is not easy because often it means great inconvenience for people who have moved away. The board and the membership must be convinced that it is a part of their Christian witness to remain. Members who oppose the decision should be urged to withdraw from the church so that their will does not prevail as a disruptive force within the membership itself.

Once this decision is made, a committee should be appointed to visit the families that have moved in. A specific radius of blocks surrounding the church should be marked off and all of the persons within the designated area should be called on and given a personal invitation to attend religious services. It is important here to say that this first invitation should not be to come to a church supper or to some charity affair that is for the benefit of the immediate community—no, the invitation should be to share in the experience of the worship of God. Wherever there is a promise of attendance or an interest on the part of the newcomer, the committee member should endeavor to make it definite, even to the extent of saying, "I will be waiting on the steps, or if it's raining, in the foyer of the church to greet you when you come." This means that when the persons who are new in the neighborhood attend the service for the first time, they will feel that there is at least one person in the church who will know them, recognize them, and make them personally welcome. When the service is over, there are certain people whom the visitor should meet: the minister, certain of the lay leaders of the congregation, and any members of the immediate family of the person who called upon them in their home. To go beyond this is to make of the visitors a kind of exhibit and it carries with it the feeling that too special an effort is a sign of condescension.

If there are children in the families, these children should be invited to the church school. Here the church must help its members to realize that a part of the commitment involved in remaining in the church means that their children will continue to attend the church school, even when children of another race attend. (In the early days of Fellowship Church, there were some adults who attended the church regularly, but sent their children to segregated Sunday schools on the ground that the children would not know how to handle integration experiences. Their assumption was false.) From this point on, the Christian spirit and the regular resources of the church will be enough to assure the newcomers to the neighborhood and the visitors at the church services that they may become members in good standing in the common life of the religious fellowship.

The second type of church, the white church in a "safely-white" district, brings up a question that is not often raised: How can we induce Negroes to attend services in our church and in time to participate in our religious life? The difficulty here is two-faced: the desire to have Negroes attend the church and become members may be a part of the minister's interpretation of his Christian vocation; and it may well *not* be the desire of his official board or his congregation. Such a minister may decide that the fruit of his ministry must be manifest in an inclusive religious fellowship. As long as he preaches about it but undertakes no steps to bring it to pass, there will, almost certainly, be no problem within the fellowship. Congregations are accustomed to giving their assent to what the preacher says by regarding his pronouncement merely as a sermon but not as something that is binding on their particular Christian witness. I recall one minister who felt obliged to act on his vocation. A young Negro woman and her mother who had attended the religious services under his ministry for more than a year conferred with him about joining the church. He was very much in favor, only to discover subsequently that his officers or those carrying the responsibility for presenting persons for membership, refused to recommend these two people and the minister had the humiliating experience of having to call on them and ask them to withdraw their request in order to avert a profound rift both in his official family and in the congregation.

On the other hand, a sensitive minority in the congregation may insist on inclusiveness without regard to the official attitude of the church or the rest of the membership. If this is the case, such a minority has to lay the foundation for inclusiveness before introducing Negroes who are asking to be members. This may be done in many ways: through informal conversations, through having such a question on the agenda of the program of committees or study groups within the congregation, through calling the attention of members of the church and of the congregation to what are the pronouncements of the denomination. But let us assume that all hurdles are cleared, the desire authentic, and the concern real—what then? The most obviously effective way is to find those persons in the congregation who have meaningful experiences with Negroes in the life of the community and then to move from any of these experiences to shared religious experience. This is easy to see and difficult to achieve because in the average American community most of the contacts across these lines are contacts without fellowship. The common sharing of interests, of concerns, of facing the normal vicissitudes of the human struggle with someone of another race happens too infrequently to count for much. I am profoundly convinced that it is very difficult to meet as friends before the altar of God if there is no fellowship in the market place.

Back of all of the separateness—and perhaps created by the separateness—is a simple lack of trust and an unwillingness to run the risk of humiliation. Many Negroes who would like to participate in the religious life in a so-called "white" church are unwilling, for many reasons, to take the step because they have no confidence that they will be received normally or courteously. To deal with this situation I suggest these steps be taken:

The attitude of the particular church must be clear and unequivocal.

Those members of the congregation who have normal, natural contacts with Negroes should invite them to share one more contact: the religious fellowship.

If it is known that there are Christian Negro families in the neighborhood, or a Negro family that is not active in a Negro church but is religious, an invitation should be given them to attend religious services.

If there are programs in the church other than the formal religious service to which the public is invited and if there are persons in the Negro community who by their profession or vocation would be interested in this particular kind of program, then care should be taken to invite them to come.

Experiences of unity between people are more compelling than all the prejudices that divide them, and if we can multiply these experiences over a long enough period of time, we can undermine and destroy any barrier that separates one man from another.

The problem facing the Negro church when it is confronted with the imperative of inclusiveness is not easy either to understand or to analyze. Through the years of American life the Negro church has been the one place in society in which the Negro members of the community could experience not only freedom, but autonomy. The ante-bellum Negro minister, wherever he functioned, shared one profoundly revolutionary insight with all who came under the sound of his voice. He said to the slaves, "You are somebody. You are God's children." This provided the slave with a firm foundation of self-respect which could not be destroyed or effectively undermined by any of the formal or informal violences of his environment. The role of the church in the life of the Negro has been like an oasis in a desert or a wind break behind which the community could develop a sense of belonging and a dignity which could not be found in any other aspect of his environment. The Negro church as an institution in society was unique, even in the life of Negroes. It was essentially a classless institution. I realize that in some instances this is clearly inaccurate, but for the most part the church within itself was without class discrimination. This meant that here at least a person who became a member of the church counted as a person, without regard to his status in the society. The church served as a rallying point for all of the organized life of the Negro community. The sanctuary of the church was often the only possible meeting place for public gatherings. The gatherings ranged from concerts to meetings such as those of the National Association for the Advancement of Colored People. This was the locale for all of the gatherings that had to do with the common life of the community. It was here that the members could experience a kind of freedom of expression, of thought, which was denied them in the general environment.

During the years, the role of the church in the Negro community has changed but remains essentially a haven of refuge for a minority who feel like aliens in the general social environment. When the Negro church opens its doors to the white members of the community today, there still lingers the old feeling that the door is being opened to the enemy. This mistrust and suspicion has to be prescribed for. The mistrust and suspicion in the Caucasian community arises again and again out of a lack of knowledge and a lack of understanding and a lack of contact. The mistrust and suspicion in the Negro community arises out of the experience of that group in the society. It is registered in pronounced moral and spiritual scar tissue. The result is that before the Negro church can really desire inclusiveness, its membership must accumulate experiences of inclusiveness in the general environment. When a member enjoys enough such mutual experiences he will not feel that in making his church inclusive, he is giving up the one place in the general community which gives him the so-necessary sense of protection from the subtle violences which surround him.

In the larger world beyond the neighborhood and the district, the sanctions of the white-dominated society "protect" the other white institutions by "drawing the color line," even when the law prohibits it. This is not true in the smaller world of the ghetto in which much of Negro life is lived. Nevertheless, the Negro church and the white church are under the same ethical imperative. They are both bound by the same commitment, and no extenuating circumstance can at the last be used as a permanent alibi for not obeying that imperative. The Negro church can no longer sit in judgment on the exclusiveness of the white church and at the same time be content to regard itself as immune to the same searching judgment. The great Negro denominations such as the National Baptist Conventions, the African Methodist Episcopal Church, and the African Methodist Episcopal Zion Church are under the command of God to grapple with the issue of inclusiveness as it affects their local congregations and their national conclaves. One of the great spiritual perils of a persecuted being is the danger he runs of escaping all responsibility for doing the Will of God. The organizations of the religious life of Negroes must by now have learned, by experiment, many methods and devices for achieving integration under the handicap of those who suffer most flagrantly from segregation. The Negro has a rich and redemptive heritage which must not be lost in this effort to become an integrated religious fellowship. How to conserve the essential idiom that has kept alive in the spirit of Negroes a courage and a vitality that has sustained that spirit in all of its vicissitudes, and at the same time to bring into its fellowship more and more of those who are not Negroes, until at last from both sides there is a common meeting place in which there will be no Negro church and no white church, but the church of God—that is the task we all must work to finish.

FELLOWSHIP CHURCH

The Church for the Fellowship of All Peoples

THE COMMITMENT

I affirm my need for a growing understanding of all men as sons of God, and I seek after a vital experience of God as revealed in Jesus of Nazareth and other great religious spirits whose fellowship with God was the foundation of their fellowship with man.

I desire to share in the spiritual growth and ethical awareness of men and women of varied national, cultural, racial, and creedal heritage united in a religious fellowship.

I desire the strength of corporate worship through membership in The Church for the Fellowship of All Peoples, with the imperative of personal dedication to the working out of God's purpose here and in all places.

www.ingramcontent.com/pod-product-compliance
Lightning Source LLC
Chambersburg PA
CBHW051106160426
43193CB00010B/1332